COPYCAT

BY VICTOR COSTA WITH CRISTINA ADAMS

COPYCAT

A FABULOUS (AND SLIGHTLY NAUGHTY) MEMOIR OF A LIFE IN FASHION

atmosphere press

Published by Atmosphere Press

Cover design by Felipe Betim

Atmospherepress.com

For my wife, Jerry Ann, whose beauty, grace, wit, and good taste caught my attention and my heart all those years ago

TABLE OF CONTENTS

La Dolce Vita
October 2021

Part One: The Boy from Liberty Road
1935-1958

Part Two: New York
1959-1973

LA DOLCE VITA, OCTOBER 2021

It's another humid day in Houston. Swollen gray clouds punctuated by erratic strobes of sunlight make it feel more like June than October. A perfect time to be indoors at River Oaks Country Club with three hundred of the city's most fashionable ladies. The ballroom foyer is awash in sartorial splendor as guests mingle and chat over glasses of chardonnay, browsing the posh pop-up shop from Neiman Marcus and a display of mannequins in vintage couture. Across the packed room, there's a live auction featuring a brand-new Ferrari and a raffle for luxury gifts. It is a sumptuous tableau of the good life. The very good life.

Above the buzz of the crowd, one of the organizers draws raffle tickets and calls out the winning names. Delighted cries of "That's me!" or "I won!" rise above the din. From my position in the wings, I watch as wave after wave of well-dressed women stream into the ballroom to claim a seat at their assigned tables. The abundance of affluence spread among the thirty or so tables is remarkable: ladies dressed in Chanel, Dior, Oscar de la Renta, Gucci, Versace, Armani, Saint Laurent, and more as far as my eye can see. Flower-festooned hats, elegant handbags, and string after string of pearl necklaces. So much beauty makes me sigh with pleasure.

I spy a couple of Victor Costa designs—my designs—and blink a few times to keep from tearing up. The Italian Cultural & Community Center is honoring me, a kid from the Fifth Ward, with a fashion show and luncheon. All these people showed up for me. Sometimes I want to pinch myself to make sure I'm not dreaming. The luncheon co-chairs signal that it's my turn to take the stage. I adjust my tie, take a breath, and step out from behind the curtain to exuberant applause and a standing ovation. I am overwhelmed by the attention; by the focus on my contributions to fashion. Odd, because I've always run toward the spotlight, not away from it, but today there's a hint of doubt, of hesitation, hanging around. At moments like these, which are admittedly rare, I'm reminded of where I started and how far I've come.

With a smile and a wave, I welcome the guests, share a couple of funny stories, and serenade them with one of my favorite Italian arias. As I sing—I've always enjoyed putting on a show—I marvel at my good fortune. I am eighty-five and still—after all the good times and misadventures, successes and failures, regrettable decisions and those that have filled my life with joy—wonder how I got so lucky. Then I think, *You worked for it; you busted your ass for it.* Holding that thought close, I finish the first aria and continue with a second one about love, happiness, and the good life. And I smile.

PART ONE:

The Boy from Liberty Road, 1935-1958

CHAPTER 1

The house I grew up in wasn't always a happy one. My parents fought like alley cats. Like Italians. My father would tell my mother that he stopped by a coffee shop for a piece of pie on his way home from work, and she would accuse him of flirting with the waitress. Their bickering would escalate to shouting in two different languages, my father in Sicilian and my mother in Italian. Listening to them was like being on a roller coaster, terrifying and thrilling, although I never really understood what the argument was about. But I knew it wasn't good.

At the time, I couldn't fathom why and how these two people, who hardly went a day without picking a fight, put up with each other long enough to say "I do" and have a family. To me, it seemed like a miracle. But the truth is the motivation was probably more practical. Because it was 1927 and she was the oldest daughter in an Italian family, it fell to my mother to care for her younger siblings. She could either babysit her brothers and sisters until the youngest grew up and moved out, or she could find a husband. Not much of a choice if you ask me, but those were the cards she was dealt.

So, on a sunny afternoon in 1929, redheaded, green-eyed, intrepid Mary Candelari married Rosolino "Russell" Costa, a swarthy, handsome Sicilian immigrant with a fourth-grade education. If nothing else, he was her ticket out. Who could blame her? As a married woman, she left her parents' crowded household to become empress of her own.

Escaping is a theme that runs throughout my family tree. My father left Sicily for America, and my mother eluded spinsterhood by marrying him. My older brother, Donald, escaped into sports and was around only at mealtime and bedtime. My younger sister, Eva, became a nun at the age of seventeen in a solemn, well-attended ceremony marking her union with Jesus. And while I admired her tenacious devotion and willingness to deny herself some of life's glorious pleasures, I thought at the time that she was, in her own way, taking a powder. As for me, from the first time I sketched a movie star dress for my paper dolls, I knew I was destined for something more. Exactly what, I wasn't sure. But something bigger and better and, most importantly, somewhere else.

I was born in 1935, a week before Christmas. At the time, my parents and my brother lived in a house on Lindale Street in north Houston. The house was small, but it was theirs; the neighborhood was tidy and working-class. But when I was an infant, we left that house and moved across town into an apartment on Liberty Road in the city's Fifth Ward. Down the street was a sprawling railyard and a creosote treatment plant. My memory has lost names and dates over the years, but the coal-tar stink of creosote that permeated the neighborhood day and night has stayed with me like a tacky souvenir.

Families like mine were scarce in that part of town. The Fifth Ward was a well-established black neighborhood with businesses and schools that had been around for years. As a child, I didn't think anything of it. But in the 1940s, segregation was the norm—in stores, churches, restaurants, everywhere—and among our neighbors, we stood out like five white thumbs. It would have been awkward if my grandparents weren't already living there.

You may wonder why we left the comfort of our house for a three-room apartment. In a word, family. My mother's parents had a spacious house on Liberty Road where they had raised all eleven of their children. At some point, they—really my grandmother—decided to open a store. Rather than buy an existing building, they converted the first floor of their house into the store and moved upstairs to the second floor. We're talking the mid-1920s, so it was more of a general store, not a shiny, state-of-the-art supermarket. My grandparents lived upstairs and worked downstairs. Once my grandfather died, my *Nonna* managed things on her own for a while, with help from her sons.

I never met my grandfather. By all accounts he loved to drink and sing, in that order, and didn't much care for restocking shelves. After the attack on Pearl Harbor, my uncles enlisted and went off to fight in the war, leaving my grandmother to manage things on her own. That didn't last long. When *Nonna* asked for help running the store, my mother—whose sense of duty to family was matched only by her excellent taste in clothing—said yes. The three rooms behind the store became our new home.

A couple of years later, my sister arrived. That handful of rooms was cramped quarters for three kids and two adults. The place had a few necessities: beds, a toilet, and a table where we ate our meals. The list of what it did not have—a refrigerator, hot running water, and a washing machine, among other things—was conspicuously longer. We stashed our eggs and milk in the store's meat case and bathed in a metal washtub that my mother filled with water she heated on the gas stove. Bath time was a lot of work, which explains why we only took two or three baths a week. Our clothes, however, were probably washed more thoroughly than we were. Never one to be outsmarted by a lack of anything, my mother used a big-bellied cauldron she kept in the backyard to boil our laundry clean. One of the most vivid and oddly cherished memories I have is of my mother standing over the cauldron, stirring sheets and towels with a long wooden paddle.

Without those modern conveniences, our home life sometimes felt like a pioneer wagon train. My parents even kept a few pigs in a fenced-in area on the far side of the backyard. By the time I was seven, it was my job to slop them once a day. Neither of my parents ever admitted to culling the herd, but I noticed that the meat case filled up with bacon and ham steaks whenever their numbers dwindled.

Like good Catholics, we attended mass every Sunday, if only because my mother insisted on it. For all her wonderful qualities, Mary Costa was not a woman to be trifled with. She had a ferocious temper and didn't hesitate to beat us with a strap—or whatever she could get her hands on—if we misbehaved or talked back. My brother, sister, and I knew better than to cross her. So we showed up at mass, scrubbed and polished, and never whined about getting up early on the Lord's day of rest.

During the week, the sisters at Holy Name grammar school supervised our religious education, along with more mundane subjects like reading and writing. They shepherded us from class to the playground to lunch and back to class; some even kept a ruler handy in case students needed a reminder of who was in charge. It was there, during recess, that my nascent career found a toehold. The playground was divided into two sides by gender. The line between them was a demilitarized zone patrolled by suspicious, sour-faced nuns to ensure the unspoken rule that girls played with girls and boys with boys wasn't bent or broken.

I disagreed with that rule. I wasn't being rebellious; I didn't like the way boys played. Chasing balls and knocking each other down was not my idea of a good time. I preferred to play with the girls because they wanted to see my paper dolls and the clothes I drew. Because I wasn't only copying what I saw in the movies, I was also drawing from my imagination.

Before long, I had so many requests for paper doll clothes that I spent all my recess time on the girls' side. With a pencil and a box of crayons, I sat and sketched outfits worn by Betty Grable or Joan Crawford and sold them to my classmates for a nickel each. It was much more satisfying than a game of kickball. Of course, when the nuns found out what I was up to, they put a stop to it.

"Boys and girls don't play together, Mr. Costa," Sister Michael, one of the playground border guards, scolded me. "We remind you constantly, but you continue to flout our rule. If you don't want to play with the boys, you will stay inside during recess."

Thanks to Mrs. Knox, a generously proportioned fourth-grade teacher with a towering beehive hairdo and a smattering of freckles across her nose, my exile became an exercise in productivity. When the nuns banished me indoors, Mrs. Knox parked me in a classroom where I could draw every day while the other kids played outside. That was my kind of recess. Where the nuns found me odd for not wanting to roll around in the dirt or play ball, Mrs. Knox saw the value in encouraging me to do what I loved. I didn't think I was so strange. Apparently, neither did she.

Like the nuns, my father didn't know what to do with me. A metalworker at a local company, he was strong and fit, and worked long hours at a physically demanding job. When he wasn't working, he loved to watch and play sports. My brother, Donald, played football, baseball, and basketball as soon as he could run, while I drew dresses and flowers and listened to "Let's Pretend" on the radio every Saturday morning. We were opposites, about as different as two brothers could be. Is it any surprise that my father preferred Donald's company to mine? I should have been hurt, but instead I was relieved that Donald had the necessary ingredients to be the kind of son my father wanted. As I got older, what little patience I had for my father's inability to bridge the gap between us began to fray. He was, after all, the adult; I expected more. Hindsight being crystal-clear, I admit I wasn't very nice to him. If I had to do it over, I'd try harder to find some compassion and an olive branch.

My mother, on the other hand, adored me. Maybe too much. Maybe to make up for my father's lack of interest. I wouldn't be who I am without her, and I certainly get my innate sense of design and style from her. Mary Costa loved beautiful clothes and had exceptionally good taste, cultivated from the pages of *Vogue* and from her pre-marriage job as a salesgirl at a clothing store that offered deep discounts in the front and, for the more intrepid shopper, a trove of designer lines in the back. It's where she said she learned to appreciate the virtues of well-made clothing. From the time I was little, she took me with her whenever she went shopping.

On Friday afternoons in particular, we would stroll up and down Main Street to admire the displays at Sakowitz, Battelstein's, and Everett Buelow. She didn't shop often, but when she did, she usually spent at lower-priced stores. That said, she did love to reconnoiter at the more elegant retailers and, once in a long while, splurge on a pair of shoes, a blouse, or a stylish haircut from the pages of *Harper's Bazaar*. I educated myself while she browsed or tried on clothes, flipping through the ladies' magazines while I waited to give her my opinion. All these years later, images from those magazines remain fresh in my mind. My first exposure to women's fashion opened a door that has never closed.

Despite her fondness for fine clothing and for me, my mother wasn't a sugar-and-spice kind of woman. Every Friday after we did our window shopping, it was time to do business. An entrepreneur ahead of her time, my mother held the lease at a former mansion on Travis Street downtown and sublet the rooms—the dining room, living room, bedrooms, even the six-car garage—as individual apartments. It was 1945; soldiers were coming home from the war, they needed places to live, and housing was scarce across Houston. My mother collected the weekly rent on Friday evenings like clockwork, with a loaded pistol in her purse because her tenants paid in cash. She would knock on the door and say, "Rent is due. Give me the money or get the hell out." Like I said, she was a tough cookie. By the time she finished, she had a wad of bills in her purse.

On the corner of the property was a billboard promoting the Metropolitan and Majestic movie theaters. New films always opened on Fridays and ran for only a week, so a night at the movies was considered a big deal. My clever mother offered the theater owners billboard space for their ads in exchange for two tickets to the movies every week. Once she was cashed up with rent money, we would head down Main Street to Christie's Seafood, order a fried shrimp dinner for one dollar and twenty-five cents, and finish in time to make the ten o'clock show. Those Friday evenings were a gift, precious beyond measure—I understood that even as a boy. What I couldn't have foreseen was how a glimpse of Joan Crawford gliding across the screen in a black evening dress would change the course of my life.

In another place and time, my mother would have run a company—or commanded an army. But in the 1940s, she made do with what she had, motivated by the desire to move up in the world and out of our three rooms in east Houston. The creosote treatment plant down the street, while a blight on our neighborhood with its steady stench of smoke and tar, employed a lot of people at a time when reliable employment was a precious commodity. Where there were jobs, there were people with money to spend at my mother's store. On payday, she waited at the gate to the plant and as workers walked out with their paychecks in hand, she offered to cash them so they could pay their bills. She extended store credit to people who had none, introduced layaway plans, and arranged low-interest loans for big-ticket purchases like refrigerators.

To an outsider, my mother must have seemed like a compassionate business owner giving the less fortunate a leg up. But she was a businesswoman first, and when it came to business, she was sharp as a needle and ruthless, too. Her wrong side was a place you wanted to avoid. Those who made a late payment or missed one altogether soon found out what it meant to incur the wrath of Mary Costa: store credit revoked, loans put on hold, privileges suspended until everything was paid up. My mother didn't suffer fools and no-accounts with much goodwill. I like to think her redhead's temper had something to do with it.

One Christmas, I asked for a doll. Not a big baby doll, but a smaller doll the size of Barbie, who didn't exist yet. I wanted a doll I could dress in outfits I drew. My parents wouldn't buy me one, so I made my own. First, I sketched the face of a pretty girl on a bedsheet. Then I cut it out, stuffed it with cotton, and tied it at the bottom with a ribbon to keep the stuffing from falling out. Finally, I glued rope curls on top for a blonde Betty Grable hairstyle and scrounged for scraps of material to make clothes for my new, three-dimensional doll. I was about eleven years old and had no idea how to sew. I'd never even threaded a needle. But I had officially graduated from paper dolls to the real deal, so change was in the air.

My father thought I was a sissy for wanting to make clothes and play with dolls, and he didn't hesitate to show his dismay with the occasional comment or worse. I remember one afternoon—it must have been a Saturday—I was sitting on the floor of the bedroom I shared with my brother, surrounded by crayons and bits of fabric, drawing clothes to make for my doll. I heard my father calling for me. He walked in, saw what I was doing, and, without any warning, gave the doll a kick. The toy flew across the floor and under the bed, leaving a trail of cotton stuffing in its wake.

"What kind of boy plays with dolls?" he growled, pointing at my pile of fabric scraps. "You should be outside playing ball with your brother. Boys don't play with dolls, girls do. No more dolls, Victor!"

Whatever I said to him has been lost to the fog of memory, but I remember bursting into tears and dragging my doll out from under the bed, only to find her seams torn loose. I also recall that my mother came in to see what the commotion was about, saw me crying, and turned her temper on my father. From there, it deteriorated into yet another fight between my parents. While they were yelling at each other, I slipped outside with my battered doll and patched her up with a few safety pins.

My mother probably agreed with my father that I shouldn't play with or talk about dolls, if only to avoid being terrorized on the playground by the class bullies. Unlike my father, however, she kept her opinions to herself—maybe to spare me, or maybe to spare herself the embarrassment of having to explain my interest in dolls to friends and family. In any case, she took a softer approach. She knew I was going to find a way to play with the doll no matter what, so she treated it like a special activity. Something to be done at home.

"You want to keep your dolly safe, don't you?" she would say. "How about you play with her at home and only at home? She can stay in a drawer during the week, nice and safe, and you can bring her out on the weekends. How does that sound?"

My clever mother. It sounded fine to me. What did I know? I was a child. But I knew enough to hide the doll where my father would never look, and I only played with her when he wasn't around.

As a youngster, I loved singing almost as much as I did drawing. Anytime I had the chance, I would open my mouth and let it rip. The sheer joy of singing—well, there's nothing else like it. I sang at home, at school, at church, everywhere and anywhere, and apparently well enough that the organist at my school requested me for the Holy Name Church choir. Mrs. Benarito, a woman who wore expensive shoes and expensive clothes and drove a fancy car, heard me singing at school mass one day and went straight to the nuns with her petition. "We don't have any sopranos to speak of," she told the nuns. "That boy sings like an angel. I want him on Sundays." That's how I wound up standing on a wooden box, shoulder to shoulder with adult choristers at the eleven o'clock mass. I was the happiest kid in east Houston.

It wasn't long before the attention piqued my mother's interest. Friends encouraged her to find a teacher to nurture my talent; the idea of voice lessons began to take shape. At that time, there was a show hosted by Mrs. John Wesley Graham on KPRC radio called *Stars of Tomorrow*. If you were lucky enough to take voice lessons from Mrs. Graham, you were invited to sing on the show on occasional Saturday mornings. It was kind of a racket because the opportunity was only available to her students, but my mother didn't mind. She took me down to Mrs. Graham's studio for an audition and signed me up for lessons on the spot. Every now and then, people commented to my mother that they'd heard me on the radio.

There was just one hitch. About the time I turned twelve, my voice began to crack and change. Where a few months earlier I'd been performing with precision and grace, puberty now made my voice unreliable, unpredictable, and, for Mrs. Graham, unacceptable. The lessons and radio appearances dried up, but my love of singing didn't. Fortunately, Mrs. Benarito didn't care if my voice was high or deep as long as I could hit the notes. I sang my heart out for her until I went to high school.

CHAPTER 2

Every family has an eccentric. My mother's sister, Amelia, was ours. A redhead like my mother, she was the kind of person who, if you left her alone too long, might run down the street naked for the sheer pleasure of it. She loved to dance and laugh and have lively conversations with herself. My relatives talked around her quirky behavior in hushed tones, chalking it up to Amelia being kicked in the head by a horse when she was a little girl. I never understood why. Aunt Amelia may not have been playing with a full deck, but in my book she was certainly the most entertaining member of our extended family.

"She isn't like the rest of us," my grandmother used to say. "She's an angel."

"How can she be an angel, *Nonna*, if she's still alive?" I demanded an explanation and got shushed with a scathing look from my mother.

Even Aunt Amelia's taste in men was offbeat. Her boyfriend was rumored to be a low-level gangster who moved from Chicago to Houston under mysterious circumstances. And he walked with a limp.

"Vincent said he was shot in the leg and run out of town," I overheard my mother tell my father one night. "They say he drove off in the middle of the night with a duffel bag, and was told to never show his face in Chicago again. Can you imagine? Do you think it's true?"

"Who says that? A bunch of gossips with nothing better to do," my father said. "And who cares if it's true as long as he makes her happy and doesn't shoot anybody."

From my eavesdropping spot behind the bathroom door, my heart raced. My head hummed with nervous excitement. What had the gangster done to deserve exile? Murder? Robbery? Extortion? The possibilities were thrilling!

Aunt Amelia met him at a large family gathering—a friend of a friend of a friend kind of thing—and it wasn't long before courtship began and love bloomed. He showed up with flowers; she mooned over him. He came to Sunday dinner at my grandmother's house. He smoked cigars with my uncles. For all I knew, he and my aunt ran around in the middle of the night, naked, by the light of a full moon. They were a strange yet perfect match. There was only one snag: marriage was out of the question. It turned out that when the gangster left Chicago, he also left behind a wife. So while his love for my aunt sparkled like a three-carat diamond, he was a strict Catholic who subscribed to the unspoken, age-old custom that infidelity was acceptable, but divorce was not. That left them with two choices: live in sin or go their separate ways.

Their decision to move in together must have shocked Italian grandmothers across Houston to the toecaps of their old-country shoes. If anyone else in the family had done something so audacious—it was the 1940s, after all—there wouldn't have been enough Hail Marys to get them into the hereafter. But addled Amelia, who, in hindsight, was probably crazy like a fox, got a pass.

The gangster and my aunt owned Gigi Liquor in the Heights and lived behind the store in a two-story yellow clapboard house on Yale Street. Compared to my family's three rooms, their house felt like a palace, with enough room for a family of five and a couple of pets. But they had no children, so I was occasionally invited to spend weekends with them. The gangster adored kids, especially me as I was a happy-go-lucky youngster, always singing and eager to please. Weekends at their house were magical: delicious meals, my own bedroom, lavish attention. *"Do you want to go to the movies, Victor?"* and *"Listen to his voice! Sing us another song, Victor!"* and *"What would you like for dinner, Victor?"* and *"Draw me a dress like Joan Crawford's, Victor."* You get the picture. What was not to love?

On Sundays, when the gangster drove me back to Liberty Road, he would give me a pat on the head and a parting gift of a few dollars, sometimes even five or ten, which was a lot of money for a young boy. "This is for you, Victor." He smiled. "Think of it as an investment in your future. Save it and spend it wisely." I took his advice and squirreled the money away. I had no idea what I was saving it for, but the future to which he alluded lay large before me. I could be patient.

My mother had two other sisters: Annie, who was married to an Irishman, and Gloria, who was the youngest of her siblings. Aunt Annie must have heard me talking about wanting to earn money, because in 1948 she and her husband hired me to move in for the summer to look after their five-year-old son, Darrell. I was thirteen years old, heading into high school, and eager to add to the savings I kept hidden in one of my dress shoes. Aunt Annie worked all day at Gigi Liquor, and her husband worked at the Houston Ship Channel; my job was to entertain and feed Darrell during the day and have dinner ready when his parents came home from work. Out of necessity, I already knew how to cook a few dishes, so putting dinner on the table wasn't a problem. I spent that summer making pasta sauce, helping my cousin with his reading, and playing outside when the weather permitted. For all that, I made ten dollars a week.

That doesn't sound like much by today's standards, but for me it was like winning the lottery. When I moved back home at the end of the summer, I had a fat roll of bills to stuff inside that dress shoe. I was eager to spend some of it, but on what? I decided I wanted clothes. Not any old rags, but classy, well-cut clothes I would be proud to wear. These days, it's not unusual for teenage boys to follow fashion trends or pay attention to their appearance. But when I was that age, what boys wore was dictated by their parents, not Instagram influencers. Fortunately, my mother and her impeccable eye for style steered me down a different path.

A week before school started, I walked into Sakowitz, an elegant department store on Main Street, and went straight to the men's department.

"Do you have any Tina Leser shirts?" I asked the sales lady.

"Of course we do, young man," she answered, peering over the counter at me and no doubt wondering how I could possibly know anything about the pioneering sportswear designer. "Who are you shopping for?" Her tone rang high and haughty.

"They're for me," I said, sharpening my tone to meet hers. "I have the money right here." And I pulled some cash from my pocket, waving it under her nose like smelling salts. Even at the dawn of adolescence, I didn't like being talked down to.

After some back and forth, during which I convinced this buttoned-up woman with a pointy nose and a round, lacquered hairdo to take me seriously, I spent a few wonderful hours trying on shirts and admiring them (and myself) in the mirror. I remember the clouds of perfume as I drifted past the cosmetics counters, the elevator operator perched on her wooden flip-down stool, the well-groomed salespeople standing guard on the second floor. But my sharpest memory is of the clothes, an endless expanse of men's and women's, casual and tailored, cotton and broadcloth, gabardine and silk and faille, elegant for evening, sober three-piece suits, gowns to make you swoon. It gave me a sudden, fierce jolt of pleasure, the likes of which I had never experienced. When I finally left the store clutching my precious haul of two shirts in a shopping bag, I understood for the first time that not only did I love clothes—I wanted to *create* them. For real women, not paper dolls.

I got my first chance just a few months later, when my mother's youngest sister, Gloria, announced she was getting married. My mother assumed the role of commander-in-chief (as she often did), marshaling every detail of the wedding, from what the bridal party would wear to what food would be served at the reception in the banquet hall on Little York Road. Aunt Gloria did not have the money for a posh wedding dress, but that didn't stop her from aspiring. One Saturday, she and my mother announced they would spend the afternoon at some of the city's finest department stores so the bride-to-be could try on a few gowns, for inspiration if nothing else. They invited me to come along. I think my mother recognized by then that I had an eye for color, form, and fit, that I knew instinctively what set one piece apart from others on the rack, why one blouse could trace the lines of a woman's frame while another hung limp like a granny's housecoat. And I had a knack for remembering how something looked, down to the dispensable details.

That afternoon, my aunt tried on gown after gown at different stores until she found one at Battelstein's that made her squeal, "This is the one!" when she looked in the mirror.

It was a luxurious gown that mere mortals like Aunt Gloria couldn't hope to afford. But it was "the one," so my mother decided her baby sister would have it. Which meant that I would copy it. That night, I went to work, sketching it from memory: the sweetheart neckline, the chapel-length train, the delicate beadwork. A week later, we took my sketches to a black dressmaker named Honey, who said she could make the dress for a fraction of the retail price. We bought satin in the fabric department at Levy's and beads from a wholesaler my cousin knew. Honey made the dress according to my sketches, stitching every single bead on by hand, and turned out a gown fit for a princess. I was thirteen years old, and Aunt Gloria's wedding dress was my very first copy.

The bridesmaids were a different story. Aunt Gloria had four attendants, including my mother. She liked what I did with her wedding dress so much that she asked me to design dresses for her bridesmaids. What I came up with was simple: a long-sleeved lace top with a full drop-waist skirt made of netted tulle. We splurged on a copper-colored Chantilly lace for my mother and Aunt Annie; for the two younger bridesmaids, I took the skirts and created a pouf-like effect with layers of blush-tinged beige satin and tulle. I even designed open-crown tulle hats framed with roses for each bridesmaid to wear down the aisle.

Aunt Gloria and Vincent were married in February 1949. I wanted to be in the wedding; I wanted to wear a tuxedo and be part of the pomp and circumstance of the occasion. But Vincent, my aunt's future husband, insisted on his nephew being the ring bearer and my sister the flower girl, so I was relegated to a seat between my father and my brother. I wasn't happy about it, but I soothed my bruised ego with the knowledge that the bride and bridesmaids were wearing my dresses. My first copy and my first original designs. In the end, it was a lovely affair.

My aunt's wedding proved to be a defining moment for me. *The defining moment.* As I watched Honey stitch together panels of fabric with the help of a sewing machine, it dawned on me that dresses weren't just pictures in a magazine. They had to be made, and that involved finding fabric, measuring, fitting, cutting, and more. It was great to have an eye for detail and color and form, but who cared if you didn't understand the mechanics of dressmaking? I didn't have a sewing machine and didn't know how to use one. But I did have a small fortune burning a hole in the sole of my dress shoe. Maybe, like the gangster said, it was time to invest in something.

A couple of months after the wedding, I took the bus downtown to the Singer Sewing Center to look around and possibly buy a sewing machine. Good thing I'd saved most of my earnings because even back then sewing machines weren't cheap. I wandered the aisles; I gaped in wonder at the spool pins and flywheels, needle bars and bobbin winders. With the help of a patient saleswoman, I finally chose a slant-needle Singer, which also came with a bridge table and six lessons with a lady named Mrs. Alma Brown. Every Saturday morning, a group of us met upstairs in a balcony area overlooking the store. There, over the course of two hours, I learned the ins and outs of using my machine—how to thread it, how to hold fabric straight and feed it through, how to oil the innards. Even now, I can see her standing over me during one of the first classes, shaking her head.

"Victor, it seems you have sewn your shirttail to that yard of practice fabric," she said, sounding not at all surprised. "Please undo the stitches and try again. But first tuck your shirt in."

It took every one of those six lessons for me to get comfortable with my Singer, but once I figured out what knowledge I was doing, I was hooked. I hauled that twenty-five-pound machine with me whenever I moved—to New York, Paris, and back to New York—every time thinking, *Surely, this will be the last move. Surely, it won't survive another trip.* I would unpack, set it up, and turn it on. A few angry snorts later and we were in business. Things went on like that until sometime during the Nixon administration, when the Singer finally cranked out its last stitch. Just when I'd begun to think it might last forever. But in 1949, I was a rookie itching to make pretty clothes. I told my mother I wanted to set up a sewing studio in the garage and was surprised when she didn't put up a fuss. She probably figured it was worth sacrificing a little garage space to keep me happy and out of trouble.

CHAPTER 3

That year proved to be life-changing. Not only did I have a new sewing machine, but I was also navigating the brave, new world of high school. St. Thomas High School was—and still is—an all-boys Catholic school with a passion for sports. When I joined the ranks of freshmen, my brother was a junior there, already well-established as a social guy and a star athlete. I knew this going in, just like I knew that I would not be playing any sports if I didn't have to. Being chased and tackled by a mob of boys who outweighed me by thirty pounds sounded tedious and painful. I wanted nothing to do with it.

Every year, St. Thomas had a huge influx of ninth graders, so many that the school divided us into different classes, A to D. I wound up in the A class, where I didn't know a single kid. Worse yet, I had Father Allnock for Algebra. The priest and longtime teacher was famous for his love of competitive sports, especially football, so I shouldn't have been surprised when he called on me during the first week of class to discuss his favorite sport and whether I would follow my brother onto the field.

"Stand up, Mr. Costa!" he boomed from the front of the classroom, his round, middle-aged face lit up with something like glee. "Let's have a look at you. I see you're built like your brother. Maybe not as tall, but you'll make an excellent addition to our football team nonetheless." Back then, you could say things like that, and nobody thought anything of it. To him, it wasn't a question of whether I would join the team, but which position I would play.

Father Allnock went on to wax rhapsodic about St. Thomas's annual football triumphs against bigger, wealthier, *non-parochial* schools, stopping short of evoking a David-versus-Goliath scenario. I pasted a neutral look on my face and tuned him out, thinking that once he was done with the rah-rah speech I would sit down, and we'd go on to tackle that day's quadratic equations. It wasn't until the boy in the desk next to mine cleared his throat that I realized Father Allnock had stopped talking. Twenty-one pairs of eyes stared at me, apparently waiting for a response. Nobody warned me this might happen.

"Um, thank you, Father," I said, not sure if he expected me to give some kind of Academy Awards-style speech. "You're right, Donald is a terrific athlete, but I've never been good at sports. I'm sorry to disappoint you, but I won't be playing football."

The words barely made it out of my mouth before Father Allnock, apparently offended by my lack of athletic skill or enthusiasm (or both), picked up a chalkboard eraser from his desk and threw it at me with the force of an aspiring Major League pitcher. The felt rectangle came at me like a torpedo, hitting me just above the right eyebrow. I let out a yip—don't let anyone ever tell you that being walloped by an eraser doesn't hurt—and a thin stream of blood began trickling down the side of my face.

Thanks to the priest's keen hand-eye coordination, I ended up at the doctor's office getting stitches; more than seventy years later, you can still see the scar. Father Allnock, on the other hand, probably ended his day with a cup of coffee in the teachers' lounge and a clear conscience.

Other than the occasional unpleasant encounter with a stiff-backed priest, high school was marvelous. I loved going to class, the energy and anticipation of a school day stretching out before me, the raucous laughter echoing through the hallways. I met boys who shared my interest in singing, theater, and literature, and I made friends. Like me, most of the boys at St. Thomas came from different Catholic schools and neighborhoods, some well-heeled and some—like mine—stubbornly working-class. And then there were the boys who lived in River Oaks.

A neighborhood of great wealth and grand homes, River Oaks was the doorway to a world of power brokers, business tycoons, politicians, and society hostesses with housekeepers and tasteful wardrobes. Or so I thought. Because I gleaned all my information about the neighborhood and its residents from the gossip pages of the *Houston Post*, it's no wonder I built it up in my mind to be Shangri-La. I was right about one thing, though: compared to where I lived, River Oaks may as well have been Mars. And Mars sure wasn't what I was expecting when my new friend, Bill Anderson, invited me to come over one day after school.

I wish someone could have snapped a picture of me when we pulled up in front of his house. One of *those* houses. In River Oaks. What did my face betray? Surprise? Awe? Barefaced envy? The front yard was a lush, vivid green carpet of ryegrass; imposing live oaks and Southern magnolia trees ringed the lawn's outer edges. On either side of the front door stood an oversized planter brimming with purple and white pansies, and the flower beds were filled with azalea bushes set to bloom a riot of fuchsia in early spring.

"You live here?" I sounded skeptical, but what were the odds?

"Sure do." Bill grinned, opening the door and waving me in. "My mother will be down any minute. She's usually here when I get home from school."

The foyer gave out onto an elegant living room appointed with a velvet sofa and a couple of wingback armchairs, ceramic table lamps, antique side tables, and a large Persian rug. Beyond that, a pair of French doors led to a patio and a sprawling backyard, complete with more azalea bushes and a swimming pool. I was so dumbstruck by my surroundings that it took me a minute to notice the woman descending the wide spiral staircase. Bill's mother wore an aqua-colored hostess gown that wafted behind her like a royal train; her copper-colored hair was swept up and lacquered in place. She floated down the steps, graceful and smiling, and my heart stuttered for a beat or two. I didn't know if Mrs. Anderson dressed like that every day—for all I knew, she'd been upstairs nursing a gin martini—but at that moment, she was a vision in chiffon, like something out of a movie. This wasn't Shangri-La; this was so much better. So much more. I didn't know much about this world of hired help, cut-crystal vases filled with fresh flowers, and abundant leisure time, but now that the door had opened long enough to offer me a glimpse, I wanted in.

One of the first things I did freshman year was join the Glee Club. I loved singing at home and in the church choir, so why not at school? Before long, I was auditioning for plays and musicals. Not only could I deliver lines from *Macbeth* with all the angst of a tortured Scottish lord, but I could also croon a Toora Loora lullaby to make Bing Crosby weep. Down deep— or maybe not so deep after all—I was a performer in search of an audience. It wasn't long before I became a regular on stage, often singing and dancing with girls from St. Agnes, who were imported to play female roles.

One of my favorite productions was the annual Bat and Ball Varieties, a follies-style show held downtown in the Music Hall. One year, I performed a duet with Thamer Sacco, a St. Agnes girl whose father was a doctor. We hit the notes in "The Desert Song" with just the right amount of misty-eyed yearning and got a standing ovation. But our voices weren't the only stars that night. At a lobby reception after the show, Thamer told me how many people complimented her dress. "All the girls want to know where I got it. One of the mothers asked if I went to Sakowitz or Battelstein's," she laughed. "And

I said, 'No, I went to Victor Costa's garage.'"

Halfway through freshman year, between Glee Club rehearsals and homework, I started designing and copying clothes. Word got out that I could sketch the dresses in *Vogue* from memory and, before I could say "Let me take your measurements," a gaggle of St. Agnes girls were knocking on my door. So I sketched designs—copies and originals—for free and then took them to be cut and assembled by a woman named Miss Adamo. There were more talented and more affordable seamstresses like Honey, who made my Aunt Gloria's wedding dress, but if you were Italian, you usually went to Miss Adamo, the undisputed queen of dressmakers in the Italian community.

Don't get me wrong, she had decent dressmaking skills, but she was essentially a mechanic. All the dresses she made looked alike, with slight variations on the theme. For a hundred dollars, which was a lot of money in those days, your daughter's wedding dress would end up looking like your next-door neighbor's daughter's prom dress. That's what you got when you went to Miss Adamo: a straight-up, A-line dress with a few sparkles here and there, maybe a bit of lace if you were lucky. Solid construction, no imagination.

Knowing the same fate awaited the dress I designed for Thamer, I spent an afternoon with Miss Adamo explaining what it should look like.

"This piece of lace is asymmetric. See?" I said, moving fabric panels around and arranging the lace on top at an angle. "It won't work if you float it on one of your usual patterns. It's not an A-line. You have to put it together like this so it turns out like that." I pointed to my sketch.

Her irritation was obvious, but I didn't care. I instructed and insisted, cajoled and railed. In the end, she made the dress I wanted, probably so I would go away and leave her in peace. It was the only time she accommodated me. My next sketch fell victim to her cookie-cutter style, as did the next one and the one after that. That continued for several months: me spelling out in extravagant detail what to do and how to do it, only to have her produce the same tired garment over and over. Then one day, I delivered a design for a dress that called for lots of material in different colors.

"What is *that*?" she said, pointing to my sketch with the kind of revulsion you'd reserve for a large, hairy insect.

"These are layers of netted tulle, Miss Adamo," I said. "There are seven layers. You start with this color and go all the way down. Seven layers, seven colors. Here are all the swatches and the names of the stores where I bought them."

On my way out the door, I heard her muttering to herself words like "complicated" and "ridiculous." So I wasn't surprised when my mother informed me later that day that the doyenne of dressmaking wanted me to steer clear.

"Victor, what is going on with Miss Adamo? She called me this afternoon very upset. 'Mary, your son can't come here anymore. He causes too much trouble,'" my mother said. "'He wants things his way, not the way I make them. He wants seven layers of tulle! I don't have time for that. I make my dresses, I charge one hundred dollars, and that's all I do.'"

My mother arched an eyebrow at me, hands on her hips. It was a pose that implied nasty consequences for the wrong action or answer. Anger rumbled around deep inside me. I wanted to shout my outrage down the street, to the entire neighborhood, in one long, thunderous roar. Instead, I surprised myself by laughing.

"Miss Adamo has a lot of nerve, Mama," I said. "She doesn't want to make anything except the dresses she always makes. Trouble only happens when I ask her to do something different and follow my design. But the girls keep going to her, so she doesn't change. She doesn't have to."

"What are you going to do about it, Victor?" My mother crossed her arms, tapping a shoe on the concrete floor—*tak, tak, tak*—a move that signaled expectation. I thought about it for a minute.

"I guess I'm going to stop asking Miss Adamo to make my designs," I said slowly. "I can sketch and sew, so I guess I'm going to make them myself."

My mother nodded, the hint of a smile curling her lips. In that moment, I made up my mind: I was sick of settling for second-best. If Miss Adamo could make money with her stale ideas, I could do better. My dresses would be spectacular.

I was sixteen, running a (very) small business, and doing well in school. I had a full life, with friends and interests and occasional weekend plans. I was lucky—I knew that—but I wasn't satisfied. Every morning when I opened my eyes, the first thing I thought of was how much I loathed our teensy, jam-packed apartment, the funk of creosote that hung on every branch and breeze in the neighborhood. On this subject, I was a shameless malcontent; I took every opportunity to squawk with noisy insistence and exclamation points. *It's too small! There's no privacy! I have to take two buses to school if I miss getting a ride with Donald! The neighborhood smells bad! We don't have a shower! It's uncivilized!* It wasn't fair to compare our meager resources to those of my wealthy friends, but I couldn't help it. They had shiny, two-story, four-bedroom homes and two-car garages; we had two bedrooms for five people and no hot running water. I resented the hell out of all of it, but we were tethered to Liberty Road by economic circumstances; I was stuck there until I finished high school. Or so I assumed. Turned out I was wrong. Mightily wrong.

I've always had a knack for finding things, even when I'm not looking for them. Especially things that don't want to be found. Such was the case one afternoon when I stumbled across a small fortune hidden under my mother's wedding dress. Thanks to an allergic reaction, I was home from school, covered in itchy red hives that my mother kept dabbing at with a paste of baking soda and water. Too miserable to read or draw, I went into my parents' bedroom to rummage around in the trunk at the foot of their bed, where my mother kept her trousseau. I wanted a closer look at the beadwork on her dress, maybe for inspiration or relief from the boredom of being trapped at home.

When I took the dress and veil out of the trunk, I accidentally lifted the wood shelf beneath, which turned out to be like a false bottom. What I saw stole the breath right out of me. Under the shelf lay a pile of money. Tons of cash right there in our apartment. I counted it, of course, every single bill until I reached a final tally of thirty-thousand dollars. All this time, my parents had a small fortune hidden in our apartment.

"We're living without hot running water, and you have all that money in there." I came out of their room furiously waving a fistful of cash. "We could buy a house with this, for crying out loud!"

My mother may have slapped me for shouting, but not before she informed me that they had been socking money away to do exactly what I suggested: buy a house. Several months later, my parents purchased a lot on Durness Way behind St. Vincent de Paul Catholic Church in a neighborhood called Braeswood Place. Their original plan was to buy a house they'd seen advertised on television, but by the time they got around to looking at it, the architect had sold it.

Never one to take "no" for an answer, my mother hired a builder to track down the architectural plans for the model house and build it. Which he did. How did our new house compare to the place on Liberty Road? It was like a waking dream. Like night and day. On Durness Way, we had three bedrooms, two bathrooms, a dining room and a living room with a modern round wall, a sliding glass door, and floor-to-ceiling windows, which were a unique feature in those days. My mother called it our wall of glass.

During the construction phase, it was my job to take two buses out there after school and oversee the progress, since both of my parents worked and my brother was in college. Once the house was built, we had to furnish it. Not surprisingly, we didn't have much good furniture; in fact, we had very little furniture at all. Before we moved in, I went with my mother to Suniland Furniture, a high-end store where all the elegant ladies and their decorators shopped back in the day. Together, we bought choice pieces of Baker furniture—a serpentine sofa with an ottoman, armchairs, side tables, and a dining room set—and, like gangsters, paid cash for everything because they had enough money saved to buy a house and furnish it. We went to Sakowitz and emerged with decorative accents, a pair of exquisite lamps with pagoda-shaped silk lampshades in pink, green, and navy, and hand-painted wallpaper for the living room. I was like a boy in a very expensive candy store.

A new house also meant new responsibilities. When we finally moved in, I was a sophomore in high school. Unlike many of my classmates, I knew my way around a kitchen, so my mother charged me with putting dinner on the table every night. If that's what it took to stay on Durness Way, I was happy to do it. I was never going back to Liberty Road—you could have it on toast. Every afternoon, I did homework and prepared a meal that was warm and ready to serve by the time my parents and sister walked through the front door.

Truth is, I became quite a cook, in no small way thanks to Jane Christopher, who hosted *TV Kitchen*, one of the first television cooking shows in Houston. Years later, when I was a designer on the rise, she asked me to stop by and whip something up on her show. Just for a moment, in front of that live audience, I was a high-school student once again, making beef stroganoff and daydreaming about a future I couldn't wait to live.

CHAPTER 4

Leaving Liberty Road for the lush suburban wonderland of Durness Way changed my life. From the first night we spent in our new home, everything was different, upended in some ways I could have predicted and later in ways I never saw coming. Like a truck speeding through a red light, I barreled straight into my future without a thought.

We had only been in our new house for a few days when I first saw the girl who would eventually become my wife. I was sixteen years old, a naïve high-school sophomore whose biggest transgression until then had been gyrating my hips a little too suggestively during my solo rendition of "Ballin' the Jack" at a Glee Club Concert the year before. I didn't know from sexy back then; I just moved my body the way Gene Kelly did when he performed the same song. If he could do it, so could I. The priests at St. Thomas weren't impressed. The morning after the show, I was summoned to the principal's office for a lecture on propriety and virtue. I didn't understand what all the fuss was about. In my short life, I had pined for only one girl, Charlotte Romeo, whose knowledge about the unspoken rules of flirting, teasing, and social banter far outclassed mine. The truth is I knew next to nothing. I was an inexperienced boy overcome with adoration for a girl who only had eyes for seniors. No way could I compete with their biceps and swagger.

Charlotte Romeo was vaguely on my mind the day I saw Terry for the first time. I was riding my bicycle past St.

Vincent's when I saw a crowd gathered in the yard outside the church. A band was playing on a stage, and girls danced around a maypole in time to the music. At one end of the yard, a group of ladies sold cookies and slices of cake. At the other end, nuns poured glasses of iced tea. Deep in the crowd, a couple of priests practiced public relations with their parishioners. I stopped to watch the May Fete scene unspool before me on that bright spring day, when all of a sudden there she was: a girl with silvery blonde hair wearing a lacy white dress and a crown of cornflowers and daisies. She took my breath away, this radiant May Queen. I couldn't stop staring at her. Any stray thoughts I had of Charlotte Romeo vanished like a balloon into the blue sky. I walked my bicycle closer to get a better look. I couldn't stay—there was homework to do and dinner to cook—so I memorized her face, her smile, the shine of her hair, hoping I might run into her somewhere. At church, the library, or the soda fountain at the local drugstore. By chance or lousy timing, we didn't meet that day, but I never forgot that first missed encounter. Who knows how things would have turned out if I had just kept pedaling?

Funny how your future finds you when you least expect it. Summer came and went, and I was a junior in high school, back to the usual routine of homework, chores, and kitchen duty. I was busy from the time I woke up to the moment I fell into bed, but I thrived on the hustle and energy of my time-starved schedule. I've never been good at sitting still and doing nothing. Not long after school started, I joined the choir at St. Vincent. I had aged out of voice lessons with Mrs. John Wesley Graham by the time I was twelve, but my love of singing only grew as my voice deepened and found its range. I sang in the Glee Club and in theater performances at school, and now I sang in the early service on Sunday mornings at St. Vincent, where a forty-something-year-old man named Mr. Tschumy and I made up the entire tenor section. He could really sing, which surprised me. I didn't think people his age could sing or dance or tell jokes without embarrassing their children.

Despite the age gap, Mr. Tschumy and I became choir pals. We talked before rehearsal and after Sunday mass. Over several months of singing and socializing, I gave him a brief rundown on my life—that my family had recently moved to the neighborhood, that my mother ran her own business and I was a student at St. Thomas. While there wasn't much to tell since I was only sixteen years old, I tried to make us all sound worthy of an audience. Mr. Tschumy, on the other hand, had a full life to talk about. I learned that he worked as a salesman for the Mosler Safe Company, that he and his family lived in a house near Rice Institute (now Rice University), and he had a son and a daughter, who was a freshman at St. Agnes. One day, after choir practice, he invited me to their house to meet her.

"She's going steady with an older boy, and her mother and I don't like him," Mr. Tschumy said as we stood in line to turn in our sheet music. "We want her to call it off, and you seem like a decent young man."

"Yes, sir," I said, dumbfounded. What was I supposed to say? Some people would have taken offense at being scouted for the position of teen escort, but I didn't mind. As far as I knew, they were from the right side of town, which meant they probably had a nice house and money to spend, and that suited me just fine. What could possibly go wrong?

We agreed that I would stop by the following weekend for lemonade and a soft introduction. Early Saturday afternoon, I took off on my bicycle for University Boulevard, eager to get a good look at some of the capacious homes that ringed the college campus. I hoped one of those houses might be my destination, but as the numbers on the address markers got bigger, the houses got smaller. By the time I found the Tschumys' house, my hope was flat as roadkill. It was nothing special: a small one-story brick affair with a handful of struggling azalea bushes in front. Nothing at all like the palatial home I'd envisioned. I parked my bicycle on the front porch and rang the doorbell, cheered by the prospect of lemonade and a short visit.

When the door opened, I almost fainted. Surely my mind was playing tricks. I blinked a few times. Nope, I wasn't hallucinating. There she was, the May Queen from St. Vincent, standing in front of me, blushing and fresh in a full-skirted, blue-and-green plaid dress with a cream-colored Peter Pan collar. I opened my mouth and...nothing.

"Are you Victor?" she said. "I'm Terry. My dad said you were stopping by." Her voice, low and womanly, caught me off guard.

"Yes, hi, I'm Victor Costa," I croaked and held out my hand. "Mr. Tschumy and I sing in the choir. It's very nice to meet you."

It was all I could think to say. The look she gave me lasted only a beat, but it conveyed disinterest better than any off-hand remark. We shook hands and went inside to meet, as it turned out, much of her family. Her father, mother, brother, and grandmother, whom everyone called Nonni, were waiting for me. Terry obediently passed around a plate of cookies while her mother filled a tray of glasses with lemonade. I sat in the living room, a glass in one hand and a cookie in the other, while her parents asked me about my studies, my hobbies, my goals for the future. It felt like an interview.

After about an hour, they all excused themselves to other parts of the house, leaving Terry and me alone long enough to start a conversation. She told me about her friends, how they liked listening to Eddie Fisher and going to the movies. I made her laugh, and when she smiled the world burst into brilliant flame. She surprised and charmed me, even when she admitted to dating another boy without her parents' approval.

"Dad must like you or he wouldn't have let you near the front door," Terry said.

"How do you go out with someone he doesn't like?" I

asked. "How does *he* get in the front door?"

"Oh, he doesn't," Terry laughed. "I do what I please and sometimes I get into trouble for it."

It should have been a red flag. I should have read the signs and run, but I was lost, a sucker on my way to falling in love with the May Queen. Two hours later, she agreed to another chaperoned date. How I made it home without riding straight into a tree is a mystery.

By Thanksgiving, Terry and I were an item, as much as any two high-school kids in those days could be. We saw each other at school dances, mixers, and theater productions, and occasionally went to the movies or out for an ice cream. But most of our "dates" occurred at her parents' house, on the front porch or in the living room. Sometimes we went for a walk around the block so we could hold hands. What can I say? Terry may not have been an innocent, but I was.

Even with a crowded schedule of school, choir practice, and a new relationship, I snatched time, here and there, to design and sew. Sketching prom dresses for family friends and St. Agnes girls—while avoiding any contact with the intransigent Miss Adamo—kept me going creatively. For the first time, I began to think seriously about college and my career ambitions. By the beginning of my senior year, I had a plan.

I knew I wanted to be a designer, so I looked for colleges that offered a degree in fashion. The likely place for that to happen was New York City, where iconic designers like Charles James and Norman Norrell hung their hats, where you went if you wanted to work in fashion, where the heart, soul, and brains of the industry lived and breathed and made spectacular clothes. Where I wanted to be.

By the time I finished researching options, my very short list of schools had shrunk to a choice of two. Of those, only Pratt Institute promised a bona fide, four-year degree in fashion. Never mind that I'd never heard of it or that it was in Brooklyn. I would be just a subway ride away from Manhattan, where everything happened. That was good enough. I filled out the application, sent it off, and a couple of months later, got the news that I was in. My father didn't understand why I wanted to go so far away when there were perfectly good colleges closer to home. I was having none of it.

"You can't go and live in New York by yourself," he announced over a family dinner not long after I received the acceptance letter. "Why don't you apply to Rice Institute like your brother?"

"I'm admitted and I'm going," I said, looking him square in the eye. "Write the tuition check and let's get on with it."

I wasn't always the most respectful son; more often than not, I felt like I was speaking a language my father did not understand. I could wax for hours about color and texture, the challenges of working with lace and the trick to cutting fine silk, while he preferred to discuss baseball stats and potential draft picks for the Yankees. But our differences and emotional distance were no excuse for treating him like an unwanted pest. He could have refused to pay—I don't know why he didn't. If I had to guess, I'd say that the prospect of me moving far away held some appeal. That, and my mother would have made his life hell. As for my relationship with Terry, we agreed to keep things going long-distance. What did we know? We were teenagers, and she still had two years of high school ahead of her. But we were in love, which, of course, trumped everything.

Like an exquisite French pastry, love has a thousand layers. My love for Terry was youthful and dreamy, with a sort of Romeo-and-Juliet quality to it. Young lovers kept apart, in our case, by geography. My love for New York was all-consuming, passionate. I couldn't get enough of everything the city had to offer; I ate it up—as much and as fast as I could. I watched and worked and learned, both in the classroom and out in the city. I didn't want to miss a thing. In 1954, New York was the capital of American fashion; to me, it felt like the center of the universe.

Pratt didn't have much in the way of residential space for students back then. Most of us lived in houses that had been converted into makeshift dormitories. That first semester, I shared a room with two other boys on the second floor of a large two-story house a couple of blocks from campus. The house was owned by Mrs. White, a bosomy widow who smelled like Aqua Net and tobacco. Her hair, which she pulled back in a tight bun, was stiff as a two-by-four and the color of dryer lint. She also had a short, hot fuse, but she charged students reasonable rent and didn't poke around in our business. Because we didn't have a kitchen—imagine bedrooms, living rooms, dens, even laundry rooms transformed into dorm rooms—we ate our meals at the school cafeteria, where the food was scary on a good day. Anemic, canned vegetables, mashed potatoes plopped on a plate with an ice-cream scoop, mystery meatloaf immersed in a viscous white sauce—we all lost weight that first month.

Since I was capable in the kitchen, I took matters into my own hands. One evening, I borrowed a hotplate, whipped up the family recipe for spaghetti with tomato sauce, and invited my roommates to share a real Italian dinner. The other residents must have heard us groaning with pleasure because when I cooked again a week later, a few dinner-crashers showed up at our door asking for some of whatever smelled so good. The next time I cooked, a line of students snaked down the hallway to the stairwell. Before long, I had turned hunger into a side business; for twenty-five cents, anyone in our rooming house could enjoy a plate of my mother's spaghetti.

Growing up, my siblings and I spent a lot of time with my mother's family. There were aunts and uncles and grandparents and cousins. Lots of noise and fun. Not so with my father's family. He had a brother in Houston and a sister who owned a peach orchard in Marlin, Texas; we rarely saw them and my father didn't encourage me or my siblings to get close. We didn't understand why, but we didn't question it either. There was also an older brother he'd mentioned a few times in that hushed voice people use to speak of unpleasant things. I was reasonably sure there were more Costa relatives out in the world—in Texas, California, Boston, who knew? I wasn't optimistic about our chances of finding out. Then, one Saturday afternoon during my freshman year at Pratt, that changed. Mrs. White rang the telephone on our floor and asked for me.

"Your cousin is here," she barked.

"My cousin? Are you sure, ma'am?" I said. "I don't have family in New York."

"You do now." Her voice grew to a shout. "Says his name is Nash. Get down here! I got better things to do than hang around my front door."

I hurried downstairs, if only to prevent a scene that might bring my fellow boarders into the hallway. Standing in the doorway was a man who looked to be in his thirties. Swarthy like a Sicilian, he had a full head of coffee-colored hair, a day's worth of stubble, and a paunch you could balance a tray on.

"You Victor? I'm Ignazio, Joe Costa's son." He held out a hand, flashing a wide, pearly smile. "Call me Nash."

You could have knocked me over with a grissini. The man had a Brooklyn accent so thick you could spread it on a cracker, and he could have passed for a gangster if it weren't for his deep smile lines and impressive girth. And his father, Joe, was the uncle we had never met. Apparently, when the four Costa siblings arrived in Galveston, Texas, from Sicily, Joe headed for the Northeast, where he settled down in Brooklyn, married, and, rumor had it, went to work for the Mafia. He also had two sons, one of whom served time in prison. But I didn't know any of this at the time my cousin Nash showed up.

"How did you know where I was?" I asked, shaking his hand.

"Uncle Russell called Pop and told him you were here going to college," Nash said. "He said you were working real hard and could probably use a home-cooked meal. Pop called me, and here I am."

"Well, gosh, it's nice to meet you," I said, feeling a little off-kilter. "Would you like to come in?" I could smell Mrs. White somewhere behind me, hovering in a haze of Pall Mall funk.

"Actually, I'm here to invite you for dinner," he laughed. "Our place isn't too far, and my brother and his wife live downstairs from us. A few minutes that way." He gestured to his left.

A home-cooked meal sounded like a fine idea. This guy had all the right details about me and my family, so I figured he was who he said he was. I ran upstairs to get my winter jacket and heard Mrs. White shooing Nash out the door.

"You should call first next time," she growled. "These college boys are very busy."

I was busy all right. Busy keeping up with school, sketching new designs, working in the shoe department at Martin's three nights a week to pay for books and food. But after that first visit to Nash's apartment, where I met his brother, Tony, and their wives and children, I added dinner every Sunday with these new family members to my schedule. They were loud and generous and reminded me a little of Aunt Annie's gangster boyfriend. During the year and a half I lived in Brooklyn, they welcomed me as if I'd always been part of their fabric, and I stepped into their family meals like a hand sliding into a Cornelia James calfskin glove. As if the extra chair at the table had been set aside just for me. We didn't have much in common—Nash worked at a shipyard and Tony drove a delivery truck—and they asked me more than once why I wanted to be a women's clothing designer.

"Do you make clothes for men too, Victor?" Nash asked over dinner about a month into our Sunday night routine. "Men need clothes. Especially the Wall Street types. I bet you could make a lot of money selling them your clothes."

"I thought only fairies worked in fashion," Tony laughed, spooning more meatballs onto his plate.

"And where do you get your information?" I asked, my tone frosty.

"From the guys down at the warehouse," he said, shifting in his chair.

"So you talk about fairies when you're at work?" I said.

"Naw, just a couple of times." He shrugged. "One of my pals says that guys who work as decorators and designers are fairies."

"Why do I want to design clothes for women?" I said, pointing my fork at him. "Because I love women, and I want them to look and feel beautiful. That's all the reason I need, and it has nothing to do with fairies."

That shut them up. As much as I appreciated the family ties and homemade cannelloni, I resented anyone questioning my career choice, especially a couple of working-class stiffs who knew less than nothing about fashion. My father never mentioned calling Uncle Joe, never asked if I saw my cousins, never said a word about any of it. Neither did I. That was the kind of relationship we had.

CHAPTER 5

One of the most thrilling episodes of my time at Pratt was the day Charles James came to visit. In 1955, the designer was a legend, referred to as a genius, and popular with socialites, heiresses, and actresses. At a time when the country had slim pickings in the way of homegrown haute couture, his gowns like the Swan, the Butterfly, and the Four-Leaf Clover were inventive, unique, impractical, and extraordinary. He may have been born in England, but his creative spirit found its spark—and fame—in the U.S. I knew his work from fashion magazines, and I thought everything he designed was a work of art. When I was in high school and making prom dresses for the St. Agnes girls, I copied some of his most distinctive features—bustles, trains, close-fitting sheath silhouettes—and incorporated them into my own designs. It was a little bit of cheating and a whole lot of sincere flattery.

One day, our Apparel Design professor announced that Charles James—*the* Charles James—was planning to stop by the following afternoon, and we should be ready to present our portfolios. He planned to review them, select one that showed promise and creativity, and then discuss it with us. He came, made some small talk, and turned to the stack of twenty-five portfolios on the professor's desk. He went through them in fifteen minutes and, when he was finished, chose mine. My portfolio was, in many ways, an homage to the great designer, with page after page of tulle-layered gowns, merry widows, and floor-length skirts adorned with flowers, bows, and beading—gowns with volume and pomp.

Most of my East Coast classmates laughed at my designs; they didn't get the importance of grandeur. The idea that a gown could shine, could trumpet its arrival, could be as elegant and exquisite as the woman wearing it—that idea flew right over their heads and out the window. But Charles James understood. He talked to the class about why my sketches spoke to him and what they had in common with his own efforts to elevate women's fashion. At the end of class, the professor asked me to stay so he could snap a picture of me with the master couturier. I remember looking straight into the camera, standing next to Charles James and feeling like the luckiest guy in the world.

Years later, I couldn't help but wonder if he singled out my work not only because it was good, but also because I was young, handsome, and one of three men in that class. Charles James was married, but his fondness for young men was a big, public secret. It wouldn't have mattered to me either way, as long as he chose me.

In December, halfway through my sophomore year at Pratt, I packed my clothes and my sewing machine and transferred to the University of Houston. I'd been in New York for a year and a half and, while I loved the school and the city, I was homesick. I was tired of cafeteria food, and I missed Terry, whose picture was tacked above our communal bathroom sink. Some people would say I was crazy to leave—they were probably right—but back then we didn't have smartphones or email or FaceTime. Even access to long-distance lines wasn't a sure thing. Every phone call to Terry or my parents cost money, which meant that we only talked every couple of weeks. I loved New York, but Houston was home, even though I knew I didn't really belong there.

As soon as I settled back into my parents' house and registered for classes, I started looking for a job. A few weeks later, I was hired as a part-time salesman at Becker's Fine Jewelry downtown, working some afternoons and every weekend. There were things I loved about this job, not the least of which was that I had to dress presentably—coat and tie—for the upscale clientele and the pay was decent. But it wasn't enough. With college expenses to cover, clothes to buy, and regular dates with Terry, I needed an extra source of income. So I did what came naturally: I set up my sewing machine in the garage once again and put the word out that I was back in town and designing dresses for twelve dollars apiece. I didn't have to wait long. A couple of months after I started working at the jewelry store, I heard from Angeline Saragusa, a friend of my mother's, with a request on behalf of her daughter, Rosanette—or Rose to friends and family.

"Rose has a date with a very wealthy young man named Harry Cullen," Angeline said. "You have to help us. He's taking her to a black-tie gala, and she needs a special dress."

Harry, who had just graduated from the University of Houston, was taking Rose, a freshman, on a second date. They were attending an elegant evening affair, which required an elegant frock. The date was a big deal. Love was in the air and, according to her mother, Rose had nothing to wear.

"Miss Adamo won't let me into her workshop," I said, referring to the woman who had been making dresses for Houston's Italian girls for who knows how long. Too long.

"The hell with Miss Adamo," Angeline snapped. "I want a fabulous dress, I want it in a week, and I want *you* to make it."

Who was I to argue with that? I set aside whatever I was working on to focus on designing a dress to captivate young Harry Cullen, whose family fortune came from oil. Once I confirmed that Rose had a merry widow I could use as the foundation for the dress, the three of us went shopping at Sakowitz. Somewhere in between handbags and ladies' hats, I spied a glass case filled with silk roses in every shade of pink, from subtle blush to bold fuchsia. Right there, the dress came together in my head.

"I want you to buy me four of these roses," I said, pointing to the flowers. "The pale pink ones."

"At twenty-five dollars each?" Angeline said, eyes wide. "They're very expensive."

"Look, buy me these flowers and I'll make Rose the prettiest dress you've ever seen," I said, steering her toward the display case. "Harry will find her irresistible, I promise."

To be honest, any young man would have been lucky to get one date with Rose, never mind two; she was, and still is, a beauty with brains, good manners, and understated spunk. But I figured her mother needed more carrot and less stick. A little persuasion and Angeline bought the roses.

"I'm trusting you, Victor," she said in a voice that sounded eerily like my mother's. "This dress had better be worthy of my Rose."

For six days, Rose came over every evening and sat on a crate in my parents' garage while I worked like a mad genius to create a dress in time. First, I pulled apart two of the silk roses and sewed the petals onto the merry widow's breast cups; the overall effect was to make her bosom look like a resplendent rose in bloom. Then, I took the skirt from a white satin dress she had discovered in the back of her closet and sewed it to the petal-covered merry widow. For the finishing touch, I fashioned a pouf, like a small bustle, in pink silk taffeta, and attached it to the back of the dress, with the two leftover roses at its center. The skirt was frothy white tulle, the top was pink silk roses, and the extras were sassy but sweet. Rose and her mother loved the dress. It was a spectacular Victor Costa original.

A week after their second date, Harry left with a group of friends for a post-graduation tour of Europe. Halfway through the trip, Harry came home, just like that, and asked Rose to marry him. He said he couldn't get her out of his mind. A year after they met, they tied the knot and were devoted to each other for sixty-two years until Harry's death in 2019. I like to think my dress played a small part in their happily-ever-after.

In the fall of 1956 while Angeline was planning her daughter's wedding, my sister, Eva, informed our parents that she wanted to become a nun. Apparently, she was washing her face in the bathroom sink one morning when a voice instructed her to devote her life to God. That's the story she told, anyway. I don't know for sure, but I'd bet money that she escaped into a life of chastity and service to avoid her feelings for other women. That's not to say she wasn't devout. She was. But being a lesbian in those days—and in our family—was not an option. It already strained the rules of decency that Aunt Annie lived in sin with her gangster boyfriend; if my sister had revealed she preferred women over men, my parents likely would have disowned and shunned her. Entering the convent, even at the age of nineteen, must have seemed like a safe choice. It wasn't until after she left the convent in 1978 that she came out to me privately.

"Your sister is taking vows," my mother announced at dinner one night. "She's joining the Sisters of the Incarnate Word and Blessed Sacrament, and I want Victor to make her a wedding dress."

Most Italian families we knew were thrilled to have a son in the priesthood or a daughter in the convent. If Eva was going to become a bride of Christ, then she would have an exquisite dress to wear down the aisle with the other postulants. My mother expected nothing less. I designed a floor-length, white satin dress with long sleeves and a jewel neckline—and not much else. Was it appropriately modest? Check. Was it as dull as a headache? Definitely. My sister was walking down the aisle for the first and only time in her life; did

I really want her to wear something that looked like a night-gown? Absolutely not. I rescued that dress—and, let's be honest, my pride—with a piece of lace from a class project. First, I sewed a panel of the lace all the way around the hemline and then added a ribbon of it around the waistline. It wasn't much, but it added a little something to a very nothing garment.

I did not see my sister walk down the aisle; my parents were the only family members invited to the ceremony. According to my mother, however, the dress got lots of compliments and the wedding went off without a hitch.

A few months later, I was drafted to make yet another special dress. Except this one meant something to me because it was for Terry. Senior prom season was in full swing, and she wanted me to design a fairy-tale frock for her to wear to the St. Agnes prom.

"Make it my graduation present," she said, batting her eyes at me. "It'll be the prettiest dress at the prom."

How could I say no?

When I told one of my professors I was planning to design my girlfriend's prom dress, he suggested I make it in his class as part of the coursework. Dr. Edwin B. Roberts was my favorite professor at University of Houston. From the first day I walked into his Garment Design class, he told me in roundabout ways—and sometimes directly—that I didn't belong at University of Houston.

"Mr. Costa, your sense of scale and color is far more sophisticated than that of my usual students," he said to me one day as we walked from class to the student union. "What are you doing here, in Houston? You should be somewhere that develops and sharpens your talent, where couturiers and their muses practice their magic. In a fashion mecca, not the outback."

Dr. Roberts had flair and an easy way with words. He knew everything about the design and construction of a garment, from the basics to high-concept aesthetics, what would work and what would not, in every sense. To me, his opinion and advice mattered. That he thought I had promise was a huge, humbling compliment. I sketched up an idea and ran it by him first, then by Terry and her mother.

"We can't afford that," were the first words out of Mrs. Tschumy's mouth. "Look at all the fabric. It's going to be very expensive. Too expensive."

"Well, how much can you spend?" I asked, knowing she would lowball me. Terry's parents liked to pinch their pennies until they bled.

"We have a budget of around forty dollars," she said.

"Just give me the forty dollars," I said, not trying hard enough to hide my irritation. "I'll see that she has a dress."

"Not just any dress, right?" Terry, who had been sitting still and quiet as a stone, spoke up. "A fabulous dress, Victor. The most fabulous dress at the ball!"

If I hadn't been so in love with her, I would have walked out the front door and never looked back. All these women in my life demanded dresses that could bewitch, enchant, honor, astonish. I was all for designing for the woman; I wanted to design for many women. A dress cut well in the right fabric, with a few pleats or a specific neckline, ruffles or scallops or sequins, could make a woman look and feel like Cinderella after the fairy godmother waved her wand. Terry wanted a dress like that.

In the end, I designed a dress so magnificent I almost cried. The skirt fell just below the knee in the front and down to the floor in the back, with a layer of delicate Chantilly lace on top of the ivory tulle skirt and a train of tulle flowing from the back of the dress behind her like a river. The bodice was taffeta, also ivory, with two stand-up ruffles fashioned around the top of the bust. It was my first crumb-catcher dress, a style that comes from costume design. The cherry on top was an enormous cotton-candy-pink Victorian rose corsage from Hannah Niday, a trendy florist back in the day.

Walking into the gym at St. Agnes that night, I couldn't have been prouder of my dress and my girlfriend. They were, by far, the prettiest pair at the prom.

CHAPTER 6

I was twenty-one years old when I asked Terry to marry me. We had been dating for more than three years. Sure, we were young—Terry was still eighteen—but that's what people did back then. They got married, got pregnant, got jobs to support a family, got a house. You get the picture. A lot of getting. Besides, we were crazy about each other, and it seemed like the next logical step.

Mr. Tschumy, on the other hand, had begun to sour on me. He didn't like that I moved to New York and didn't think much of my wanting to work in fashion. Why this hadn't come up when Terry and I started dating, I don't know. Maybe he was always looking for the next shiny new thing for his daughter. Or maybe he was just an asshole.

"You know, Victor, I want better things for my daughter than a husband who makes women's clothes," he said one night, after his third gin martini. "What kind of man does that for a living? Not a real man. Are you a fairy, Victor?"

Typical coward—he didn't launch his attack until his wife was in the kitchen and Terry excused herself to the bathroom.

"No, sir," I sighed. "I am not a fairy. I love Terry."

Underneath that pure tenor voice, the man was a black-hearted oaf with about as much self-awareness as a rock. I wanted to point out that selling safes for a living made him a salesman, not a real man. I could have listed the names of designers who were both famous and successful—Balenciaga, Dior, Pucci, Balmain, and Charles James, among others—but that would have underscored his belief that fashion designers, myself included, were fairies. When he disappeared into the kitchen for more olives, I debated how and whether to stand up to him. Not only was he rude, but the man couldn't hold his liquor. Fueled by anger, I went to the kitchen door and stopped short when I heard him complaining.

"That Costa kid is nothing but a dirty wop," he slurred. "I should have never introduced him to Terry; he's not good enough for her. I don't understand what she sees in him."

At that point, I figured discretion, rather than confrontation, might keep me from getting punched or yelled at. I turned around and went back to the living room sofa. No use arguing with a small-minded, frustrated, drunk little man.

Did the memory of that evening stop me from proposing to Terry? No. In fact, I took her out to dinner, got down on one knee, and popped open a box with a marquise-cut diamond ring inside. I'd saved two thousand dollars, which was a huge sum back then, and bought it at Becker's. She said yes, and we were engaged. We didn't tell her parents right away. Instead, the *Houston Post* published our photo and engagement announcement first and then we told her parents our happy news.

Her father pitched a fit when we showed him the *Houston Post*, alternatively threatening to throw her out of the house or lock her up inside it. Her mother, a mousy woman who spent her days clipping coupons and entering mail-in contests, sat on the sofa, hands knotted up in her lap, looking worried and saying nothing.

Over the next couple months, with help from Dr. Roberts, I applied to spend my last year of college in Paris at L'École de la Chambre Syndicale de la Couture Parisienne. It is one of the most revered institutions in fashion, where couture giants like Yves Saint Laurent, André Courrèges, and Karl Lagerfeld learned their craft. All these years later, I remember Dr. Roberts's kindness and encouragement; how he guided me through the application forms and official paperwork and made sure I would get credit for the classes I took in Paris so I could graduate on time.

When the happy news came in April 1957 that I was accepted into the year-long program, Terry and I began plotting. *How often would we see each other? Should we set a wedding date? Should we get married in Houston or Paris? Where were we going to live after graduation?* In the end, it didn't matter. While I made plans to move, Mr. Tschumy was steadily chipping away at Terry's certainty about marrying me, until one day she gave in. With her father and his temper, it was often easier to run up the white flag than to keep fighting. On a rainy April afternoon, four months after the announcement ran, Terry returned my ring.

"I think Dad may be right, Victor," she said, looking past me, not at me, as we sat on the front porch of her house. "I'm too young and I don't know how you're going to make a living."

"What do you mean you're too young? You weren't too young back in December," I said, disbelief and desperation in my voice. "What's changed?"

"I'm just not ready," she said. "I'm really sorry, Victor. This isn't going to work."

And with that, she handed me her engagement ring and went inside, leaving me on the front porch, open-mouthed with shock. I imagined her father watching me from behind the living room curtains, grinning from ear to hairy ear, even though I knew he was in an office somewhere selling safes, pretending to be a real man.

Over the next days and weeks, the reality of life without Terry hit me. We had made plans, we had talked about our dreams, and overnight, *poof!*, the life we envisioned together was gone, kicked to the curb by her unhappy, spiteful father. He had bullied his daughter into dumping me, with no regard for her feelings or mine, and she folded like a tent in a high wind. The more I relived that afternoon, the angrier I got. I nursed that fury, blew on its embers, and allowed it to swell, because I knew if I wasn't angry, I might go to bed, pull the covers over my head, and stew in a mess of self-pity. I had to move forward to avoid falling apart; I had to not care—or at least act like I didn't. I worked on presenting myself as the picture of resilience. By day, I exuded an "it's-her-loss" indifference at work and school, with my friends and parents; by night, I shed the mask and often cried myself to sleep. The loss of Terry, her rejection of me, cut me to the bone.

Despite my suddenly single status, I still had one thing to look forward to: a year in Paris. The opportunity to leave Houston and all the emotional baggage behind took on more urgency. Nothing would stop me from going.

More than sixty years have passed since that first breakup with Terry. I don't remember how my parents reacted to the news that the wedding was off and I was heading across the Atlantic Ocean for a year, maybe longer. Knowing my mother, she was probably delighted about Paris—the clothes! the sophistication! the French!—and a little relieved there would be no wedding. Who knows what my father thought? Probably that I was crazy to move to a continent he had worked hard to leave.

Fortunately, Colonel Becker, who owned and ran the jewelry store, offered to refund me the price of the ring if I sold it to another customer. I polished that ring until it sparkled, put it back in the display case, and worked every day after school for a month until a young man my age bought it. Actually, his father pulled out a stack of bills and paid the two thousand in cash. A lump formed in my throat as I put the ring in the box and congratulated the future groom.

"Here you go, son," Colonel Becker said, handing me the money after closing that day. "Make sure you send us a postcard or two."

The fact that I was flush with spending money for Paris

cheered me up a little, and planning all the details of my trip kept me busy. I bought some new clothes and booked a ticket on the grand ocean liner RMS *Queen Elizabeth*. I had never been to Europe, never traveled much except to go to college in New York or visit relatives in other parts of Texas. Now I was moving an ocean away; this time, there would be no pining for my girlfriend, no phone calls or love letters. There was no girlfriend, no fiancée. A few months earlier, I thought I had my life figured out. I would study fashion design and become a designer; I would get married and have a family. And I would show people like Terry's parents—perhaps my own father, too—that I deserved respect and a firm handshake. That last part sounds a little shallow, but I felt like I had something to prove. One day there was a rosy future stretching out before me; the next, a ticket to Paris and a broken heart. Maybe, I thought, Paris would be as good a place as any to start picking up the pieces.

In the dog days of August 1957, I took a train from Houston to Penn Station in Manhattan, then caught a cab to New York Harbor. My mother had given me *Nonna*'s old steamer trunk, which had just enough room for my sewing machine, my clothes, and a Charles James mannequin that Dr. Roberts offered as a parting gift. I had everything I needed. Or so I thought. The ship was just rounding the tip of Long Island toward open ocean when I met Mary Louise Chamberlain.

"Well, hello there, is this your first time on a crossing?"

The question came from a fellow passenger standing next to me at the railing. She was lovely in her flowing, cap-sleeved floral dress and cherry-red wedge sandals, chestnut hair pinned back with tortoiseshell barrettes, and sounded like a proper lady with her refined English accent. We were among dozens of people watching the last of the coastline disappear, one shadow at a time.

"You mean crossing the ocean? Yes. How could you tell?" I said. "I'm going to study fashion in Paris."

"Aren't you the lucky one? Anticipation, that's how I know. It's all over your face." She smiled and offered her hand. "I'm Mary Louise Chamberlain, and I'm going home to London."

"Victor Costa from Houston, Texas, at your service."

I took her hand and kissed the top of it, like a royal dandy. Lord knows what possessed me to do it. Probably the sea air. Or the way she looked at me with intent. I didn't know what to make of this woman. An English rose or a Gypsy Rose Lee? She had flair and sex appeal and a certain *je ne sais quoi*, something I couldn't quite put into words. It was unnerving.

"Well, Victor Costa from Texas, don't make any promises you won't keep," she laughed, turning her blue-gray gaze back to the horizon. "I think we'll be great friends."

That evening, we went from the top deck to dinner to a more exclusive party for two. Only a few young men on the ship had private cabins, and I wasn't one of them. How lucky for me that Mary Louise had a room to herself. For six nights, we enjoyed each other's company, strolling around the ship, eating and dancing and making love until dawn. I adored her wicked sparkle and soft bosoms; she said I charmed her right out of her knickers.

Our mad, shipboard affair was the best thing that could have happened to me. By the time we docked in Southampton two weeks later, I felt almost like a new man on the cusp of a new chapter. Not exactly "Terry who?" but more like "Terry who cares?" Mary Louise and I said our goodbyes, with me promising to call if I was ever in London. It didn't bother me one bit that she disembarked into the waiting arms of her boyfriend, Phillip. She was my Florence Nightingale—she stitched me back together and then some. I was finally looking forward to arriving in Paris and finding out if everything I'd heard about French women was true. I hoped so.

*

My first few weeks in the City of Lights didn't go quite as planned. Back on the ship, when I wasn't swanning around with Mary Louise, I met all kinds of new people. In particular, older women—they were likely in their fifties, but to me they seemed ancient—took a real shine to me, probably because I held out their chairs at dinner, opened doors for them, waltzed them around the parquet dance floor a few times; in turn, they fawned over me. I have always loved women of all ages. Why discriminate?

One woman, a widow named Madame Mocondier, offered to help me get settled when we landed in Paris. Her copper-colored hair was streaked with gray, cut short, curled and coiffed, and she dressed in the innate style native to French women. A spring green sheath dress and matching duster or a fitted cream-colored skirt suit with a bright Hermes scarf draped over one shoulder—she made everything she wore look effortless and chic.

"I know a hotel that's very inexpensive, so you won't have to worry too much about money," she said. "It's ideal for a young man."

"Oh, Madame Mocondier, I don't have money for a four-star hotel room or fancy restaurant meals," I explained, thinking that her idea of cheap would be my version of first-class. "I'm on a student budget, and I'm looking for student accommodations."

She blew out a *pffft*—a quintessentially French sound that covers everything from exasperation to disinterest—and told me to collect my baggage and follow her down the gangway to a waiting car. The hotel turned out to be the French version of a motel, with rooms ranging from adequate to desperate. For not too many francs, I got a bed and a sink in a narrow room with a sloped ceiling and barely enough space for me and my possessions. I was willing to overlook the tight quarters and lack of a shower until I went in search of the bathroom, which the concierge informed me was down the hall. The toilet turned out to be a hole cut in the floor like a medieval *garderobe*. A very smelly *garderobe*. I found out later that some of the English guests referred to it as a squat-and-drop.

To celebrate my first night in Paris, Madame Mocondier insisted I accompany her and a group of friends to the Moulin Rouge. She had been so kind to me, a stranger, that I couldn't say no. What a spectacle it was: a constant flow of cocktails, a musical revue, dinner, and dancing. I don't drink alcohol—never have—but my hostess threw back a few flutes of champagne before ordering me to dance with her. As we turned and twirled, she leaned into me, brushed an invisible speck of lint off my collar, and touched my cheek. I couldn't believe it. The woman was flirting with me. If I hadn't been so tired, if she hadn't been my mother's age, I might have been tempted. Instead, I pleaded fatigue and a queasy stomach, and took a cab back to my hotel.

Needless to say, I showed up early at the student housing office on the first day of class. When the secretary asked what kind of room I was looking for, I told her anything with a bed and a toilet. Then, consulting my French dictionary, I corrected myself. "Excuse me, madame, I mean a twentieth-century toilet." For all I knew, squat-and-drops were as common here as toilets were back home. The secretary, who was not amused, found a room for me in a clean, spacious apartment on the Right Bank occupied by a woman and her son. I stayed there about three weeks, long enough to realize that the son wanted more than a garden-variety friendship. I was hanging some clothes up to dry in my room one night when he came in and said in clumsy English that he wanted to be my friend.

"That's nice," I said, feeling a little sorry for him. "Of course we can be friends."

I'll be the first to admit that I wasn't an urbane guy, and

I didn't have much experience with unconventional behavior. So you can imagine my reaction when the Frenchman took my acceptance of friendship as an invitation to make a pass at me. I let out an undignified shriek and ordered him out. Nobody talked about homosexuals back then, except to insult or make fun of them. Remember my cousins and Mr. Tschumy and their disdain for so-called fairies? I didn't know any and didn't know how to react, except to yell, "What are you doing?" He bolted out of my bedroom like his hair was on fire. That night, I slept with my door locked.

I showed up at the housing office the next day with a bouquet of flowers. This time, the secretary found a room in an apartment owned by a seventy-something-year-old widow. No husband, no children, no pets.

"*Avec une toilette,*" she said, arching an eyebrow.

I smiled and offered her the bouquet. That was good enough for me.

None of my professors spoke English. Or they pretended not to. The first day of school, I pointed and signed and made noises that sounded like questions, and they pointed and grunted answers in return until I understood what to do. Foolishly, I expected everyone—or anyone important, like professors—to communicate with me in my language. Yes, it was naïve and more than a little arrogant, but it set me back on my heels anyway when they didn't. The second surprise was the classwork. Take muslin, pull the thread, baste in the red, drape a top, and so on. The professors doled out instructions—I figured out what to do by watching the other students—as if we were slow-witted beginners with two left thumbs. I hadn't come all this way to revisit the basics. It was enough to make me wonder if moving to Paris was the worst decision of my life.

That first day, only one thing kept me from getting on the

first ship headed back to New York: knowing that visionary designers like Coco Chanel and Pierre Balmain wouldn't have put up with Sewing 101 for very long. Maybe these professors had a grand plan. Maybe they would introduce us to more complex aspects of fashion design once the less serious students dropped out. Maybe it was time for me to learn French so I could understand what was being said to—or about—me.

That's what the woman sitting next to me in Garment Construction suggested.

"I couldn't help but notice that you're struggling a bit with the language," she whispered in the Queen's English, nodding toward the professor, who was describing something—I had no idea what—in rapid-fire French. "You should invest in some lessons. The French pride themselves on not really speaking English, even though many of them know enough to be dangerous. I'm Dottie, by the way. Not crazy, just short for Dorothy."

"I'm Victor." I smiled, relieved to meet someone with a sense of humor who also spoke English. "And I don't understand most of what people around me are saying. Makes me wonder if they're having a joke at my expense."

Dottie had a pleasant, round face, wispy, shoulder-length blonde hair, and a mouthful of teeth in dire need of orthodontia. After class, we found a table in one of the college's inner courtyards and relaxed into a conversation about who we were and why we were there. She was twenty-five, married to a banker named Mark with whom she had four-year-old Jennifer. By her own admission, Dottie couldn't sew to save her life; her aspirations lay in design, inspired by Mary Quant, a rising young designer in London. I told her about my fascination with Joan Crawford and that I'd wanted to design clothing from the time I could hold a sketch pad and pencil.

"Well then, you must learn French, for self-defense if nothing else," she said, lighting a cigarette. "I went to night school at the Alliance Française. Absolutely turned things around for me. I was arriving home frustrated and weepy every day. Nearly drove my husband straight home to England."

"Are lessons expensive?" I asked. "I'm on a tight budget."

It was my lucky day. As it happened, Dottie and her husband were looking for a babysitter. Would I be interested in making some occasional money?

"You seem like a decent sort, and we'll pay well," she added, exhaling a long plume of smoke. "Worth every centime for a night out."

That evening, I signed up for classes at the Alliance Française. The following week, I became Jennifer's official babysitter. Even with the babysitting money, I struggled to cover my expenses. Sometimes I had a baguette and cheese for dinner; sometimes I skipped dinner altogether. I wasn't living in poverty, but I was living in Paris. And my parents only paid tuition and rent. Anything else I wanted, I paid for. That's how I wound up at a church potluck dinner, where I met Madame Vopel. I heard about the church from other students. They said it was run by Americans and the food was edible. That was good enough for me. On my way home from school one night, I stopped in for a look and a meal. I ate the goulash and salad, and stayed for the conversation with Madame Vopel, a petite woman with exquisite taste in scarves and handbags who apparently volunteered at the church every week. When I told her I was a student at L'École, she lit up.

"Can you really sew?" she asked.

"Oh yes, I'm very good," I said. "I've been sewing for years."

"Buying fabric is a habit of mine." She smiled, reaching into a cavernous tote bag and producing a large rectangle of navy-blue gabardine. "I just bought this today. It's Christian Dior. Can you make a dress for me?"

"That doesn't even look like a yard's worth of fabric," I said.

"But can you make a dress for me?"

It took imagination, as well as some creative cutting and stitching, but I managed to produce a pretty frock out of the Dior fabric. Madame Vopel liked it so much that she invited me for dinner at her home and insisted on making it a weekly event; I even had my own napkin. I showed my thanks by making a dress for her every now and then. It was good practice. If I was going to make it as a fashion designer, I would take on projects for food or money.

In early April 1958, Dottie and her husband were going to London for the Easter holiday and invited me to ride along, in case I wanted to go and enjoy the sights. What I wanted to enjoy was Mary Louise Chamberlain. Despite my ambitious plans for affairs with French women, I hadn't so much as held hands with *une belle femme*. I wrote Mary Louise to see if she would be available for lunch or dinner or a museum visit while I was in London.

Her response was: "Please come. I ended things with Phillip, as he has never been able to satisfy me in any way."

That was all the encouragement I needed. Well, that and the promise of her magnificent bosoms. I crossed the Channel with Dottie and her family and spent a glorious week touring palaces, the Tower of London, the British Museum, and Mary Louise's boudoir. On Easter Sunday, she went to an Anglican church and I found a Catholic one not far from my hotel. I didn't confess or ask for forgiveness, but I did say a few prayers under my breath. Just in case. The next day, I returned to Paris a happy man, blissfully unaware of how much my life was about to change.

From the minute I stepped off the train in the Gare Saint-Lazare in late August 1957, I knew I was going to fall in love with Paris. Seven months later, I still woke up every morning thrilled to be there. I was mostly enjoying school, I was making professional contacts in the fashion business, and night classes had improved my French enough that I could talk about something more exciting than the weather, which gave my social life a much-needed nudge. I had a growing rainy-day fund thanks to the money I made sewing for different ladies, and I was working on finding a job at one of the couture houses so I could stay another year or two. Or longer. Life was good and getting better.

That's when I heard from Terry. In the days before smartphones and instant messaging, travelers treated the American Express office like a bank-travel agency-post office; you could receive mail, buy traveler's cheques, pay bills, book trips and tours, and more. Like other American students in Paris, I got mail at my local American Express office. I stopped by every couple of weeks—usually before rent or tuition were due—to see if a check had arrived from my parents. One Wednesday morning, instead of the check I was hoping for, I found a letter from my ex-fiancée. It was short and chatty, designed no doubt to begin defrosting the iceberg between us.

Dear Victor, you're probably surprised to hear from me, but I was out with some girls after work the other day and one of them said something funny that reminded me of you. So I called your parents' house and asked for your address. I think your mother was surprised to hear my voice, but she was very nice about it. Did you know that I left the University of Houston? I don't think college was the right place for me. My mother says I wasn't getting much out of it because I wasn't very interested. Anyway, I left halfway through the fall semester and started working at Tennessee Gas in the secretarial assistant pool. The job is fine, and I've made some friends. Write and let me know how you're doing and whether you like living in Paris. Fondly, Terry.

I stood on the sidewalk, open-mouthed, as busy Parisians shoved past me with an occasional *"Bouge!"* snarled in my direction. This woman had ended our engagement and left me bereft and bewildered; did she really think that a cheery little note would make me forget everything she had said and done? And yet...I was curious. And flattered. Several weeks went by before I wrote her back. I kept it light, sensational- izing a few details of my life, hoping to provoke envy, regret, shock, or all three. Was it petty of me? You bet. Did I care? A little. But I didn't get the reaction I expected. Instead, Terry's second letter gushed with enthusiasm and admiration, calling me brave, adventurous, fearless. I almost wrote that I was liv- ing in Paris, not canoeing down the Amazon, but I didn't want to burst her bubble. The voice inside my head reminded me that there was a whole city of chic French women out there, even as the ice around my heart began to slowly melt.

Sporadic correspondence became weekly letters. We shared funny stories about work and school, and gossipy tidbits that might make the other laugh or gasp. Like friends.

Dear Terry: I've become friends with a pair of women in my tex- tiles and fabrics class. I thought they were best friends, but they might be a lot closer than that. I hear they're lesbians!

I couldn't have cared less that some of my classmates might be lesbians; I was thinking of my audience. Terry's teenage rebellion, which had seemed so bold at the time, was pedestrian compared to my tales of socializing with bohemians and non-conformists. I wanted to entertain and titillate.

Dear Victor: I got your last letter and loved hearing about your dinners at Madame Vopel's house and the dress designs you're working on. What a time you're having in Paris, meeting different, interesting people, even lesbians! Life in Houston is the same as when you left. The only news I have is that one of the girls I worked with was having an affair with the company's head lawyer. A married man! They were both called down to personnel, where she got fired and he did not. That seemed very unfair to all of us in the assistant pool, but what can we do? Yours, Terry.

We went on like that, back and forth via air mail, for a few months. I omitted details of my Easter tryst in London, telling her that I had stayed in Paris and attended mass at Notre-Dame. After all, my social life—or any part of my life— wasn't her business anymore. That's what I told myself, anyway. Some part of me must have known that, deep down, I was tempted to tell her everything about my life in Paris, maybe to make her jealous or maybe to prove that I was doing fine on my own; that I didn't need her.

Who was I kidding? I lied about seeing other women because I still had feelings for Terry. I couldn't be in love one day and not the next. I wasn't a light switch to be turned on and off with the flick of an index finger. But I did want to protect my heart, so I kept things light and a little flirty in our correspondence until late May, when Terry surprised me with an ultimatum.

Dear Victor, I've been thinking a lot about the mistakes I made when we were engaged, like listening to other people when I should have followed my heart. Being in touch these past few months has been wonderful. It has made me realize that I still love you very much, and I want to marry you. If you still love me, send me a ticket and I'll come to Paris. If not, I promise to leave you alone. Love, Terry.

Her letter wasn't a thunderbolt, but it got my attention. Clearly, she was ready to be a wife. As an available ex-fiancé, did I meet the requirements? Maybe that was cynical of me. Then again, we had history, some of which I did not care to repeat. The temptation to write her back and point out that she'd already blown a chance to become Mrs. Costa was a powerful one. Good thing we didn't have email or our rekindling romance would have died with a few keystrokes. Instead, I took myself to the nearest café, ordered a coffee, and pondered what to do.

That's not true. I knew what I was going to do: argue both sides and convince myself that what I wanted to do was the right thing. I spent a week thinking and taking long walks. Classes at L'École would end in June. Since I had already taken all the courses required for my major, once the school mailed my certificate of completion to the University of Houston, I would be a college graduate, free to start my career and my life.

I asked my friends for advice and got more than I bargained for. *"You're too young to get married, Victor!"* and *"Why make a lifelong commitment when you've just started to live?"* and *"Why didn't she marry you the first time? Maybe she is bored?"* and *"Don't tell me there aren't enough women in France!"* Of course, they all made excellent points. And of course I didn't listen. Who knows why, but I was ready to check marriage off my to-do list. It's what people did in the 1950s. They got married, had kids and careers. I convinced myself that I loved and missed Terry, and that we should get married in Paris. By June, we were officially re-engaged. I used most of my savings to send her a one-way ticket on the SS *Flandre*, promising that we would say our *I dos* in my favorite church, Saint-Sulpice.

Getting the priest to marry us was no problem. Once I informed him that my fiancée and I were both Catholic and wanted to marry in the Church, we just had to show up with birth certificates, rings, and a couple of witnesses. The wedding dress presented more of a wrinkle, mostly because Terry didn't have one. During our previous flirtation with prenuptials, we hadn't set a date or made it far enough into the planning process for her to consider gown styles. This time around, I offered to take care of everything. *"I'll have a dress made that's fit for a princess,"* I wrote her. *"You'll look just like Grace Kelly at her wedding."*

It was a bit of a stretch to promise that she would dazzle like the recently married movie-star-turned-princess; all Terry had in common with Grace Kelly was hair color and religion. But I knew the possibility of it, however remote, would prove irresistible as she was a devotee of celebrity lifestyles. Sure enough, she sent me a telegram saying, *"The wedding, gown, honeymoon. All yours. STOP. Be there soon. STOP."*

She arrived about ten days before the wedding. I met her at the train station with a bouquet of pink roses and whisked her off to a three-star hotel, where we dropped off her suitcases and went from there to the final fitting. The gown was nearly finished; we just needed to make sure the measurements she'd sent me were still correct. If you're wondering whether I designed and made her dress, the "we" did not include "me." A couple of audacious young women who were at school with me and moonlighted at Christian Dior made it.

Remember the lesbians? Those same girls got their hands on the pattern for a wedding dress that had been the grand finale in a Dior show the year before and smuggled it out. It was a *robe trapèze*, a kind of tent dress, from one of Yves Saint Laurent's first collections as head of the House of Dior. Ten months earlier, in October 1957, he stepped into the chief role when Dior himself died unexpectedly of a heart attack. And what a simple yet extraordinary dress it was: a tea-length ivory silk and tulle confection, sleeveless and scoop-necked with a breezy fullness in the back. My friends outdid themselves—the dress was perfection. My contribution was a tiara, which I adorned with pearlized flowers to match the seed pearls on the gown's neckline.

Terry and I were married on July 20, 1958. My best man was a friend named Jacques, who was married to an American woman named Phyllis, a stunning redhead with impeccable taste and not much money. I don't recall how I met them, but we became great friends during my time in Paris. They lived on the rue de Fleurus in a large apartment that belonged to Jacques's parents and were kind enough to invite me for dinner once a week. In exchange for their hospitality, I made Phyllis a dress every couple of months.

No one from either of our families could make it on such short notice. It was just as well. The ceremony and celebration afterward were more joyous, more fun than they would have been with her father there. Several dozen friends came to the church and then to the restaurant, where we ate, drank, and toasted to our happy future. That night, Terry and I checked into a hotel overlooking the Tuileries Garden, and the next day we took a train south to Nice, where we stayed in Madame Vopel's vacation home, free of charge, for our honeymoon. We had a marvelous time eating, sleeping, strolling, and screwing. By the time we got back to Paris two weeks later, Terry was pregnant.

There are times in life when you wish you'd known better. This was one of them. We wanted children someday, not right away, but we were too young and stupid to consider the consequences of not using birth control. I had been interviewing for jobs in Paris and was close to getting an offer at Givenchy. It would have been a tremendous experience for me in terms of learning the ins and outs of couture, but it didn't pay enough to cover rent and support a wife and a new baby. Today, pregnant women work as long as they want to, until the last minute. But in 1958, there was no question that Terry would not work. True, we were very young—I was twenty-two and Terry was twenty—but the unspoken rule still applied. She would stay home, and I would find a job. Unfortunately, we couldn't afford to stay in Paris on one income; even sixty-plus years ago, it was an expensive city. Our best option was to return to the U.S. In October 1958, we set sail for New York, with Terry three months pregnant and me unemployed.

As a student in Paris, you could go to the opera or the ballet and get great seats at a discounted price. One night while we were still living there, Terry and I got dressed up and went to an opera at the Palais Garnier. When the lights went on for intermission, I noticed a couple sitting in front of us speaking English. I also noticed that her dress wasn't buttoned properly.

"Excuse me, I'm sorry to interrupt," I said, tapping the woman on the shoulder. "The underpinnings on your dress are closed, but the buttons on the outside are undone. If you'll allow me, I can get it all buttoned up for you."

Today, that offer would probably get me a slap in the face. Not in 1958. Not only did I button up the outer layer of her dress, but the couple, Mr. and Mrs. Samuels, invited us out to the lobby for drinks. They happened to be from New York. When I told them we were moving there in a few weeks, Mr. Samuels, who owned and ran a high-end shoe manufacturing company, insisted that I call him.

"Promise me you'll call," he said. "I'm going to help you find a job."

That was all the encouragement I needed. I phoned him a week after we arrived and checked into the Hotel Albert on East Tenth Street. He insisted I come to his office, where he gave me letters of introduction to Oleg Cassini, Adele Simpson, and Bill Blass, who was then head designer at Maurice Rentner, Inc. I called, made appointments, and showed up with my portfolio. The question was always the same: "What can you do?"

"I can sketch, and I can sew," was my usual response. Really, I wanted a job to pay the rent and living expenses.

Oleg Cassini was the first one to give me a chance. He was very debonair, a count and a charming rascal who, according to gossip columnists, had slept with half of Hollywood's leading ladies. As a designer, he understood how to appreciate and dress women: pretty clothes with a bit of sex. I remember one dress he designed called Happiness Behind Bars. Hard to forget that.

"Take these swatches," he said, handing me four pieces of fabric. "What would you make with these colors and materials? Sketch me some ideas and bring them by tomorrow."

I went home and came up with five outfits for different occasions. Oleg lavished me and my ideas with praise and paid me five dollars for each. Twenty-five dollars for five sketches—that was a lot of money. But neither he nor any of the others offered me a full-time position. So I went back to selling shoes at Chandler's, which I had done during my time at Pratt. I sold shoes at night and looked for a job in fashion during the day. I also stopped by Pratt to ask about housing for former students. The school offered us three months rent-free in one of its large, pre-war apartment buildings just for signing a lease. We jumped on it and moved in.

By December, I was feeling the pinch of desperation. I had been networking and knocking on doors for a month and a half, and still no job. Maybe this was a sign that we should pack up and move back to Houston. Maybe I only thought I was a designer. Maybe I was meant to be something less impressive, like a tailor or a salesperson in the men's department at Macy's or Lord & Taylor. The prospect of failure followed me around every day like a little black cloud.

One Thursday afternoon, I was on my way to work after several wasted hours of trying to meet with manufacturers in the garment district when I stopped by the Plymouth Theatre to see if they had any cheap seats for *Once More, With Feeling*. Arlene Francis was starring, and Terry and I were big fans. It was my lucky day. There were two tickets in the high balcony, but who were we to complain? It was Arlene Francis! On Broadway! When I pulled out my wallet, the lady in the booth nodded at my portfolio.

"What's in there?" she asked. "You an artist?"

My portfolio was a huge, black rectangular case that held all my sketches. I took it with me to every meeting and job interview.

"Sketches," I said, handing her a ten-dollar bill. "I'm a fashion designer, and I'm looking for a job. I don't mean to be rude, but I need to buy my tickets and get to work."

She motioned me off to the side, gave me the tickets, and told me to wait. There were still a few people in line. Once she'd finished, she shuttered the cashier's window and stepped out of the booth. She wore a beige skirt and short-sleeved blouse with red piping—I assumed it was a uniform—and a name tag that read *Lucille*.

"Can I take a look at your sketches?" she asked, waving a hand to cut off my protest.

"Sure, why not?" I sighed. "You'll be the only person who's looked at them all day."

I opened the portfolio and held it up so she could browse the pages. There were drawings of wedding gowns, cocktail dresses, evening frocks, and daytime outfits. It took a few minutes, but she looked at every single one. And when she was done, she crossed her arms over her ample chest and looked at me over the rims of her reading glasses.

"I'm going to call somebody for you," she said. "I know a guy who does bridal. Actually, he's my cousin. His name's Murray Hamburger, and he has a showroom over on West Thirty-Seventh."

Before I had a chance to open my mouth, she was back in her booth and on the phone. A few minutes later, she emerged.

"Here's Murray's information," she said, handing me a piece of paper. "He thinks I'm crazy because I don't know you from the hot dog vendor, but I told him I liked your drawings." She paused and winked at me. "He owes me a favor."

"I don't know what to say." I looked around to make sure this wasn't a trick, that I wasn't on *Candid Camera* or something. "I really don't know what to say." That was *all* I could say.

"How about 'thank you' once you have the job?" She smiled. "Just think of me as your fairy godmother."

"How about I make you a dress if I get this job?" I asked. "I'm very good."

"I bet you are," she snorted. "Get the job first. Then we'll talk."

I rode the subway back to Brooklyn in stunned silence. I've often thought I was born under a lucky star because I really have, for the most part, lived kind of a charmed life. But that day, I had trouble figuring out how I'd managed to be in the right place at the right time.

I stopped by Murray Hamburger's showroom the following day and introduced myself as the designer Lucille wanted him to meet.

"Lucille." He grimaced, flipping through the pages of my portfolio. "She's nuts, but she has a good eye. Let's see what you can do, Mr. Costa. Sketch me a wedding dress."

Five minutes later, I handed him a drawing of the dress I'd made for Rose Saragusa the night she went to the ball with Harry Cullen, except this version had short sleeves, more layers of tulle, a satin bodice, and a chapel train.

Mr. Hamburger looked at the dress, then at me.

"You want to design wedding dresses?" he asked.

"Mr. Hamburger, I'll design whatever you want me to," I said. "My wife is having a baby, and I need a job."

"Okay, kid, you're hired," he said, handing me back the sketch. "You start on Monday. Be here at eight-thirty sharp."

"Wait, we haven't discussed salary yet," I said.

"The pay is sixty-five dollars a week," he said, pointing me toward the door. "That's what I can afford. Take it or leave it."

Of course, I took it. It wasn't as much as I'd hoped for, but it was enough to start digging us out of the financial hole we were in. A new year was nearly here, and I was finally going to work as a fashion designer.

PART TWO:

New York, 1959-1973

Mr. Hamburger knew how to cut corners and come out smelling like a rose. It's true. The bridal dresses he manufactured looked like they were made of faille—a lightweight, drapey silk fabric—of adequate quality. Instead, they were made from a less expensive, 300-denier silk normally used for lining, not dresses.

In fabric terms, denier describes the thickness of the fiber, so a 300-denier silk is heavier and less expensive than something like 70-denier faille—but it is still silk. The fabric we used was durable, attractive enough to the untrained eye, and easy to work with. We got away with using it because most young ladies (and their mothers) couldn't tell the difference, unless they knew what to look for. If someone wanted a dress that required a lining, he would order the same fabric to be cut twice, for a dress made of lining on lining. It kept our costs down, and everyone was happy. And the dresses were beautiful.

We also made dresses in different colors for all the ladies in a wedding party, and that set us apart from many bridal manufacturers, who hyperventilated at the very thought of fiddling with tradition. That's not to say that we didn't have plenty of bride-white dresses on display. Of course we did. Murray Hamburger was, first and last, a business. But a few steps deeper into the showroom revealed a rainbow of designs in rosy blush and ice-blue, shimmering peach, pale violet and ecru. Who knew that embracing pastels would be considered a bold move? Maybe my boss had a bit of genius in him, or maybe it was just a lucky hunch. Either way, the colorful dresses were a hit, and 1960 proved to be an especially profitable year for the company.

The first wedding gown I designed for Mr. Hamburger was a dreamy number in ivory with long sleeves, a high neck, lace trim around the waist, and a flowing, pleated skirt. Very feminine and old-fashioned, without being frumpy. To complete the look, I made a headpiece with silk flowers and seed pearls. The flowers, which I'd learned to make in Paris, were simple yet stunning. I took a small piece of fabric, folded it twice into two triangles, sewed it together at the bottom, and then pulled the thread through, which turned the whole thing inside out to create a lovely blossom. It was a handy little trick that never failed to impress. Once I had the dress, veil, and headpiece, I dressed a mannequin from head to hem and was relieved when Mr. Hamburger not only approved, but asked for bridesmaid dress designs as well. He liked my work, and that meant money in the bank.

A couple of months into my new job, I had the chance to design a different dress, thanks to a young woman and her mother who were in New York to see a Broadway show and shop for a wedding gown. They stopped by the showroom on Seventh Avenue early one afternoon and were cornered by the in-house senior designer, a middle-aged woman named Josephine, who, as far as I could tell, thought more of her own designs than anyone else did. In my opinion, she had no talent at all. But the woman was mean as a snake and I was at the bottom of the Hamburger food chain, so I kept my opinions to myself. My office was just off the showroom, but even with the door closed I could hear most conversations. The visiting bride-to-be sounded just this side of exasperated.

"I don't like ruffles, and I don't want the dress I see on every other model in *Brides* magazine." Her voice had a familiar twang. "I'm looking for something different, something special."

I smiled to myself. Wasn't every bride looking for that special dress? The one that would make her feel like a movie star or a goddess?

"We have some lovely samples in the back." Josephine simpered. "Why don't I pull a few and you can see if something calls to you?"

I rolled my eyes. Where had she come up with that phrase? A magazine probably, or she'd overheard someone else using it. Josephine had less imagination than a spool of thread, but she was persistent. I had to give her that. She would wear that poor girl down until she agreed to go home with a dress she didn't really want. That was Josephine's scrambled version of customer service: shove it down their throats, take the money, and show them the door.

Just then, I heard Mr. Hamburger join the conversation— warm, welcoming, always polite. Good timing or concern that his pushy head designer was going to lose a sale? It didn't matter. There was a brief discussion, with the mother's voice interjecting here and there, and then my name, loud and clear.

"Victor! Victor, are you available?" His voice, smooth, with the undertone of a summons, filtered into my office. "There's someone I'd like you to meet."

I emerged and was introduced to Marlene Nathan, whose father owned Nathan's, a famous department store in Galveston. No wonder that twang sounded like home. Marlene was lovely. I turned on the charm, and we bonded over being from Texas. That lasted about five minutes. Never one to waste much time on niceties, my boss cut through the chit-chat and asked me to design a dress for Marlene on the spot. I assumed the Nathans had money; Murray Hamburger didn't dust off his game-show-host smile for just any woman.

"A dress?" I asked, feeling a little ambushed. "Right now?"

"Why not?" he said, turning to the two women. "This one is a bright new talent, and we're lucky to have him. Nobody designs bridal like Victor."

This was an act I hadn't seen before, but I followed his cue with a nod and a deferential smile. Mr. Hamburger patted me on the back in an apparent show of confidence and camaraderie, but I knew better; I felt the last-minute squeeze of my shoulder and understood that if I didn't come up with something in the next few minutes, I could be back selling shoes at Chandler's by the weekend. Meanwhile, Josephine, who was lurking behind the Nathans, gave me a look that should have shriveled my testicles to the size of sweet peas. Lips pressed together in a wire-thin line, nostrils flaring, pupils big and black with fury, she reminded me of a bull sighting the matador's cape. She didn't lose her temper—she would never have done that in front of a customer—but I thought she might let me have it later. She didn't scare me—not much, anyway. Nevertheless, I tried to avoid being in the same room with her whenever possible.

In the meantime, I had to save my job. I grabbed a pencil and sketch pad, while Mr. Hamburger steered Marlene and her mother toward a display of bridesmaid dresses. I doodled, erased, fussed, and drew again until something took shape on the page: a long-sleeved dress with a bateau neckline, a waterfall hemline—shorter in the front, longer in the back—and fabric rose petals sewn all around the hem. I completed the look with a headpiece studded with tiny silk flowers. Not bad for an off-the-cuff design. I added a detail here and there, then presented it to Marlene and her mother.

"Here you go," I said. "We can make some adjustments, maybe in the bodice or the length, but I think this style is ideal for your shape and you're tall enough to carry a cathedral train, which would have a gorgeous, dramatic effect."

Marlene was sold before I finished my pitch. She loved it with a long string of *oohs* and *aahs* and a smile bright enough to light up a room.

"Looks like my daughter's found what she was looking for." With a half-smile playing on her lips, Mrs. Nathan turned to Josephine, who was hovering around the edge of our circle with a gown draped over each arm, and waved a hand at her. "We won't be needing those." And just like that, Josephine and her samples were dismissed.

In the end, Marlene married her college sweetheart in the dress I designed for her. From then on, I made sure to stand far enough away from Josephine that she couldn't wrap her hands around my neck and choke the life out of me. Yes, she was that awful.

Decades later, when I had my own company and showroom in Dallas, Marlene Nathan Meyerson asked me to design something for her to wear on the opening night of the Morton H. Meyerson Symphony Center. Named for her husband, who oversaw the effort to raise funds for and build the concert facility, it was the new home of the Dallas Symphony Orchestra. It was a big deal and a big night for someone I admired, so of course I agreed to pull out the stops. I had a few late nights of sketching and erasing and filling the trash can in my office before I came up with a design I thought suited her: an evening jacket embroidered with the musical notes of the night's first symphony. I don't remember the composer, but I have a vivid memory of Marlene—and the jacket—looking exquisite. Fortunately for me, the ghost of Josephine was nowhere to be found.

Once it was clear that customers liked—and bought—my dresses, I was given free rein to come up with new designs. One gown had a very plain, flat front and a full, frilly bustle so that when the bride walked down the aisle, the view from both front and back was attractive and memorable. Other styles featured a dress with a large silk rose on the bustle and smaller buds on the skirt, and one with medium-sized roses on the sleeves and trim adorned with tiny roses along the waist and hemline. Either I had a sixth sense for what brides wanted, or 1961 was a boom year for weddings because we sold more than a thousand of the gowns with the big rose bustle.

I made bridesmaid dresses as well, adding the silk flowers to many of my designs. Mr. Hamburger knew the flowers were a selling point, but insisted he couldn't afford them. What a cheapskate. I knew what our costs were and what we charged for every single dress, but I played along.

"What can you afford?" I asked him after a contentious discussion about the price of fabric.

"Not a handmade rose," he said. "The union seamstresses charge two dollars for each item. If I have to pay that, I won't make money on those dresses; I'll break even."

"Well then, how about I make these roses at home?" I said. "Pay me fifty cents per rose, and I'll make them."

Practically speaking, it was a deal for both of us—good for him and good enough for me. Every night, I took the subway home to Brooklyn with a box full of half-done roses. My sewing machine table doubled as our dining room table. After dinner, I would remove the round top, stow it behind the sofa, and get to work making roses. The next day I would turn up at work with a box of finished flowers. This routine of making ten roses a night for a total of five dollars went on for many months. I wasn't getting rich, but every dollar mattered. Terry and I had a baby coming.

It seemed to me that her belly grew overnight, every night. Maybe it happened while she was sleeping and I was sewing. Any extra cash we had went toward things like a crib, a stroller, baby clothes, bottles, and diapers. During one of our shopping excursions, I watched her waddle down an aisle of shelves stacked with infant quilts, sheet sets, and blankets. One hand on her ample belly, she made her way down the aisle, touching the fabric of a blanket or a sheet and lightly rubbing it between her thumb and index finger. I wondered how it felt, how she knew what to look for, what did or did not make the cut, what would be best for our baby.

Truth was, she didn't know, and neither did I. Terry and I were just twenty-one and twenty-three, a couple of wide-eyed naïfs who jumped into marriage, thinking it was what everyone did and it would be an easy float downstream. Instead, we found ourselves in whitewater rapids, grabbing for branches as the current tossed us around. What choice did we have but to swim?

Our son, Kevin, was born on April 17, 1959. Until that day, the greatest achievements of my adult-ish life had been moving to Paris, marrying Terry, and finding a job as a bridal designer. Overnight, everything changed. Inexperienced as I was, instant fatherhood felt like a front-row seat on a ride to a different cosmos: uncharted, thrilling, and terrifying. A week later, we left the hospital. Neither one of us remembered getting into the cab that took us back to our Brooklyn apartment, but somehow we got Kevin home without dropping him. We were dazed, exhausted, and unquestionably in love with the screaming infant who transformed us into a family. I took a couple of days off to help Terry figure out a schedule for her life as a mother and, when Mr. Hamburger called to congratulate us and let me know that he wanted a fall line by early July, I went back to work. What can I say? It was the 1950s. Paternity leave, stay-at-home dads, and remote work didn't exist. Wives had babies, and husbands made money. That's how it was. Good thing we've evolved since then.

Working at Murray Hamburger didn't come with many perks, but I did have access to a gamut of gowns and dresses, from expensive to bargain-basement. When Terry and I began planning Kevin's christening a couple of months after he was born, I reserved a time at our church, invited a handful of friends, and then filched a piece from inventory. It was a bottom-of-the-line model that sold for about ten dollars. That's right, ten dollars. Hard to imagine these days, when women often shell out many thousands (or more) for a wedding dress. I washed it, added a sample of white Chantilly lace (also swiped from the cutting room), and voilà! We had a christening gown for our son.

I used to read the *New York Times* every morning over coffee. I've never been one to form many habits, especially boring ones, but I stuck to this one religiously. I would get up early, before everyone else, and catch up on news and gossip before launching myself into the workday. It was the only time I had the kitchen to myself, and I loved it. The quiet, the stillness, the uninterrupted time. One morning, I opened the women's fashion pages to see a wedding gown displayed prominently above the fold. Next to the photo was a feature story claiming that it was an exact copy of the dress Louise Whitfield wore when she married steel magnate Andrew Carnegie in 1887. I had to read it twice to make sure I wasn't hallucinating. I knew my work, all of it, and the dress in the *New York Times* was not from the nineteenth century. It was a Victor Costa original.

"You're not going to believe this." I waved the newspaper at Terry as she shuffled into the kitchen, sleep lingering across her face. "The *New York Times* says this dress is from seventy years ago. But it's mine. I designed it last year!"

I jabbed my finger at the photo for emphasis as she read over my shoulder. Terry was pregnant again, due in the spring of 1961. Kevin, who had just celebrated his first birthday, was in constant motion, toddling around the apartment, in the park, anywhere he could get traction. I didn't know how we were going to make it work with two children—I tried not to think about how much more I would have to work to make ends meet. The thought of asking for a raise made me queasy.

"I remember this." She yawned, looking at the photo. "You showed me the first drawing you did, and I told you it was very pretty. That's definitely your dress."

"I should call and ask them to print a correction," I huffed.

I thought about that dress on the subway ride to work. I stewed in my outrage all day, as I draped, sewed, and sketched under Josephine's barbed-wire glare. By the time I got home that evening, I decided to say nothing. For now. Part of me was too chickenshit and too overextended to make a fuss. But a bigger part of me—the part I listened to in tricky situations like these—knew that Mr. Hamburger wouldn't appreciate public recognition of my dress, my design. That's the kind of man he was. Any spotlight had to shine on him and his bridal collections, not on his employees. If I said something that focused the attention on me, I'd be out of a job faster than you could say, "Make it chapel-length." I would wait for the right time. Until then, I'd keep my mouth shut.

Our daughter, Adrienne, surprised us by arriving several weeks early on March 9, 1961. She was small and wrinkled, as many premature babies are, and, yes, we worried that her little body wasn't yet ready for the outside world. But after a month of constant mothering and round-the-clock feedings, she grew— and we exhaled. I came home every night to a happier wife and a healthier baby.

Let's be honest, the times were still traditional, and we were a traditional family in the sense that, when it came to our children, Terry handled most things. When I walked through the door at the end of a long day, there was usually more work to do—flowers to sew for my day job and wedding gowns to design and make for private customers. Having money in the bank was important to me, so I worked constantly at one job, or two or three, all day and deep into the night. Working was a joy and a compulsion, one of the few habits I couldn't quit, and it came at the cost of close relationships with my children. I wasn't disengaged, but I was often distracted, thinking about the next collection or the next job search. It's something I will always regret. In 1961, however, I had my hands full with a toddler, a newborn, and a wife who had begun dropping occasional hints about moving back to Houston. It was all I could do to earn a living and keep moving forward. If only I'd had a crystal ball.

After a couple of years of working at Murray Hamburger, I decided I'd had enough. I wanted a raise and credit for my designs, and Josephine's spiteful presence was really getting on my nerves. It was time for me to exit, but I had no idea where to go. Job-hopping was (and probably still is) common in the fashion industry and, in that respect, I was no different from other aspiring designers, with an eye on the future and one foot out the door, looking for the next opportunity to move up and ahead. What I didn't know was that there was another bridal manufacturer, Pandora, with a showroom and offices in the same building. I might have found another job somewhere else in Manhattan and remained blissfully ignorant about Pandora if it hadn't been for Jerry Mantel, who owned and ran the company with his father and a woman named Maria.

I don't know where he got my name, but Mr. Mantel approached me in the lobby of our building one day and said he wanted to hire another designer. He'd heard good things about me—I was easy to work with, my designs sold very well—from various bridal buyers around town. Would I consider leaving Murray Hamburger? I agreed to meet with him and Maria. I told myself I had nothing to lose and everything to gain. Besides, it was easy enough to get off the elevator a little early. One conversation became two, then a few, and soon we were negotiating terms for what promised to be my next job.

In the meantime, I decided to call the *Times* about their mistake and ask them to print a retraction. I should have known it wasn't their mistake, that Mr. Hamburger himself told them the dress belonged to Mrs. Carnegie. But when I called, I had no idea. I wanted credit for my design.

"Your information is wrong," I told the fact-checker on the other end of the line. "I looked it up in the library and Mrs. Carnegie's wedding dress was made of gray wool with chinchilla cuffs. That doesn't matter anyway because the dress you featured with the article was designed by me, Victor Costa, in 1961."

The *Times* printed a mea culpa on a Wednesday morning, thanking me by name for setting the record straight. By two o'clock that afternoon, I was walking out the door with my portfolio, officially unemployed. Know what I remember best about that day? The wicked smile on Josephine's face.

Unemployment has never been a good look for someone like me. I am, by nature, a busy person, always moving, thinking, creating. And with a wife who didn't work and two small children, we couldn't afford for me to be jobless for very long. I sewed at home, making bridal gowns for anyone who wanted one while negotiations with Pandora dragged on. We went back and forth—What would the job entail? How much would they pay me? Would there be any perks? What about raises?—until they finally agreed to most of what I wanted. There was just one hitch: I would design only bridesmaid dresses. There was no wiggle room; I could either take the offer or keep looking.

That's the thing about working in the fashion industry. Everybody wants something from you—a job, a fall collection, special attention for special customers, more and more and more—and you have to fight to get what you want. Pandora offered me a better salary and benefits, so I took the job. For now, that was good enough. Someday, I would want more, something better. Until then, I would learn, watch, and wait.

CHAPTER 9

Most people would argue that June is the biggest month for brides. I'll concede that wedding venues do a brisk business during that first month of summer, but those who work in the bridal industry know the two seasons that matter are spring and fall. That's when showrooms fill up with future wives (and their mothers) searching for the gown of their dreams and with bridal buyers looking for the trend *du jour*, the dress that will make everyone whip out their credit cards, the dress that will sell out again and again. At Pandora, we spent summer and winter designing, cutting, fitting, and sewing to ensure we had enough inventory to carry us through the seasons. Our collections were finished and ready for public consumption before save-the-date cards were in the mailbox.

I started working at Pandora in early 1962, the same year Yves Saint Laurent debuted a collection under his own name. Those designs, which included a ladies' peacoat, sent the fashion world spinning into an ecstatic tizzy. He was called daring, a visionary leading the charge into a new era of clothing design. Fashionistas referred to him as the *dauphin*—the crown prince—of haute couture. No really, they did. Saint Laurent and I were both twenty-six that year, and it thrilled me that someone so young could soar so high in this business. I was a good designer—maybe even a damn good designer—but I knew that kind of world-stage success and celebrity probably wasn't in my future. Nevertheless, it was something to aspire to.

It wasn't long before I learned that Maria, who co-owned

Pandora with Mr. Mantel, was the primary in-house designer with her own line. Any hope I'd had of getting my name on a label went into the scrap basket. Maria had made it clear early on that I would handle bridesmaid dresses until further notice. I wasn't surprised, but I wasn't happy, either. She couldn't design a hatpin, much less a star-turn wedding gown. Anyone with two eyes and a pulse could see that.

Was I doomed to play second banana to third-rate designers for the rest of my career? Maria thought she had talent. The rest of us knew better. Even her own daughter, Caroline, who worked as our fitting model, understood her mother's limitations. Caroline was engaged to an Italian count and set to marry him in what promised to be a lavish event at St. Patrick's Cathedral, with elegant guests and mentions in all the social columns. When Maria offered to design her wedding dress, Caroline turned her down and asked me to do it instead.

Talk about an awkward moment. I didn't want to come between mother and daughter; I also didn't want to suffer the fallout of straying into Maria's territory. On the other hand, I refused to be sidelined. If I didn't advance my career, who would do it for me? Nobody. So I said yes to Caroline, and the dress I created was a masterpiece, an extravagant affair of Alençon lace, silk taffeta, and tulle. Even Maria admired the results, albeit with a sniff in her tone.

As billed, the wedding was a memorable event from start to finish. I got only the briefest glimpse of the bride at the reception, a swirl of ivory lace and silk gliding through the crowd and onto the dance floor, glowing with the happiness of a young woman in love. If only she had done some due diligence. Not long after the wedding, Caroline's new husband was revealed to be a scoundrel with a worthless title, a string of failed investments, and mistresses on two continents. It was a good reminder that when something seems too good to be true, it usually is. I should have filed that lesson away for later.

Things could have gone badly at work after that. Maria could have held a grudge. But she didn't. In fact, I was probably one of the few people she got along with at work. She had contentious relationships with nearly everyone at Pandora, especially Mr. Mantel, her business partner, and Jessica, who oversaw patternmaking and pattern design. Our meetings often gave way to the three of them arguing while I quietly sketched, waiting for them to run out of anger. I couldn't imagine how they'd worked together as long as they had. Maria and Jessica, always competing to land the next front-page design, couldn't stand each other. Maria and Mr. Mantel spoke only when necessary, and even then it was often with teeth bared. How did they ever become co-owners of a successful company?

Despite the tension and drama around the office, the job at Pandora was one of the best I ever had. It's where I would make my name as a bridal designer, thanks in no small part to Jessica. When I showed up as the new employee and bridal-wear designer, she befriended me. During my first year at the company, she taught me everything she knew about pattern design and cutting and trained me to make a pattern that could go right into production. I watched her work and learned her techniques, many of which I continued using throughout my career. What she did—what she taught me to do—wasn't easy. Still isn't. When you're making a pattern, you have to be precise down to the fraction of a millimeter, even more so when you're creating garments—like a wedding dress—that have to fit like a second skin.

Jessica suffered from digestive issues and ate yogurt every day at lunch, claiming it neutralized her stomach acid. Like Pepto Bismol. I assumed that butting heads with Maria every day was enough to upset her gut. To counter the stress of work, she took dance lessons. Twice a week, she took a bus to Arthur Murray Dance Studio to learn mambo, tango, quick-step, and cha-cha-cha. She learned all the popular dances. Over many months of classes, she became both a competent dancer and good friends with her dance teacher. In fact, she liked him so much that one day she came into work and announced that she'd convinced him to come work at Pandora. Funnily enough, he became one of the company's best pattern makers. True story. You can't make this stuff up.

After more than a year of making bridesmaid dresses, I sweet-talked Maria into letting me design a couple of wedding gowns. My favorite was an exquisite confection made with just a few yards of satin and expensive lace that repeated in six long rivers of fabric. It seemed improbable because it required so little fabric, but thanks to my design it worked. We named it the Rivers of Lace gown. A phone call led to a visit from one buyer, then another, and before I knew what was happening, Rivers of Lace appeared on the cover of *Modern Bride*. It became an overnight sensation—my first—and one of Pandora's biggest sellers. In a matter of weeks, that dress appeared in department store display windows around the country. Bridal buyers went crazy for it, reordering it over and over until the end of the season.

Unfortunately, in bridal or any fashion business, a manufacturer can't survive with one store buying one dress. That's where buying offices come in. They act as a kind of broker between the retailer and the manufacturer. Most stores—whether one store or a national retail chain like Macy's or Nordstrom—belong to a buying office, an independent company that helps them manage the merchandise they purchase. Say you're a single store in a small city in Indiana and you have a customer who needs a wedding dress. You call your buying office and say, "Mary Jane, I have a customer who's the mother of the bride, and she wants a pale blush wedding dress. I have a budget of five hundred dollars. Please find it." And Mary Jane or an assistant buyer will comb through the manufacturers they work with until they find the garment their retail client is looking for. Once they find it, they let the client know and follow up to ensure everything goes smoothly.

Any store or retail company that takes itself seriously belongs to a buying office. It was true in 1963, and still is. When I was working in the industry, department store buyers came to New York with an open-to-buy, a budget for how much merchandise they could purchase. Say the bridal buyer from Sakowitz—at that time one of Houston's most elegant department stores—came to New York with an open-to-buy of fifty thousand dollars to spend on dresses for the upcoming wedding season. She would already have let the store's buying office know her budget and what she was looking for in bridal merchandise. Before her arrival, the buying office would call around to see what bridal manufacturers and designers had available—Pandora has this, Priscilla has that, Bianchi has something else—and then share that information with the buyer, who would choose which manufacturers to visit based on input from the buying office.

As a clothing manufacturer, your hope is that buying offices will guide a variety of stores or groups of stores to your showroom. In bridal, more is better, but not always easier. Bridal buyers don't purchase a selection of off-the-rack dresses in different sizes like womenswear buyers do; they order one dress and reorder from that single piece as the need arises. Department stores and bridal salons don't keep wedding dresses in all sizes on hand. A bride might have to try on a dress closest to her size, let the salesperson pin and fuss to help her envision how the right fit would look, and then order it in her actual size. It's a more elaborate process than shopping for a cocktail dress or a pair of trousers, but that's bridal. A custom-made complication.

After the commercial success of the Rivers of Lace dress, Maria asked me to design a few more wedding gowns, some of which also became big sellers. That's when my situation at Pandora shifted. I became an asset, someone who knew what brides-to-be wanted and designed for them. For the first time since we moved to New York, I was happy. I liked what I was doing, my career was gathering steam, and life at home was as peaceful as it could be with two toddlers and a wife who thought Brooklyn may as well have been in Siberia. Did I want to be stuck designing wedding dresses for the rest of my life? Absolutely not. But thanks to bridal, I had a foot in the door to the fashion world, and for that I was grateful. Someday I would walk through it. Until that happened, I would make nice and look for opportunities.

Chiquita Williams, an editor at *Modern Bride*, once told me I had the spark of success burning inside me. I was still at Pandora, and we had just left a bridal show, heading uptown in a limousine on the way to lunch or dinner. Chiquita was a real red-hot mama with a big personality and a generous heart. Lucky for me, she loved to eat well and had an expense account to match her appetite. Free meals aside, I adored her and told her so every chance I got.

"I see you riding in limousines by yourself someday," she said as we crawled through traffic up Sixth Avenue. "Not with me or anyone else. Just you. The star of your own show."

"Chiquita, that's ridiculous," I laughed. "But thanks for the vote of confidence."

"Oh no, you've got what it takes, kid," she said. "Just remember who told you."

I remembered that conversation for weeks afterward. I remembered it when I thought about the thing I wanted more than anything but didn't have: my own line. Maria had hers, and I could out-design her blindfolded with one hand tied behind my back. I wanted a Victor of Pandora label in every dress I created. What the hell was I waiting for? Someone to hand my future to me? I called a meeting with Mr. Mantel and Maria and explained what I wanted—my own line and reservation-only shows like some of the finer bridal manufacturers—and reminded them that I had designed some of the company's best-selling gowns in recent memory. Didn't that make me a valuable asset? I thought so, and I assumed they did, too. I should have known better.

They turned me down flat. Yes, I was disappointed, but I wasn't surprised. And I didn't give notice in a fit of fury. In fact, I had a job waiting for me. A few months earlier, the company's sales manager, Nate Bernstein, left to start Bride's World, a rival bridal manufacturer. No sooner had he jumped ship than he asked me to join him. I turned him down, politely of course, because I hoped things would go my way at Pandora. Nate insisted it was a standing offer. With my design talent and his ability to sell anything, he said we could shake things up, give the bridal establishment some overdue competition.

Faced with the prospect of working anonymously under Maria for who knew how long, I told Nate I wanted more money and my own line—and I wanted it in writing. No promises made over lunch or the phone, no handshakes that could be denied. Otherwise, he could forget it. Within a week I had a contract in hand. The next day, I packed up my sketches and left Pandora.

In early 1963, anything seemed possible. John F. Kennedy was president, I was earning four hundred dollars a week, double my salary at Pandora, and I finally had my own line, Victor from Bride's World. However, there were trade-offs. Like working with Nate. I didn't loathe him, but I didn't trust him. A youthful, freckle-faced redhead, he loved to play the wide-eyed humble guy, while his father-in-law bankrolled the business. In truth, he was a canny operator who knew how to grease palms, cut corners, and turn on a brilliant smile to get what he wanted. All the magazine people loved him, which proved very good for me. I met regularly with editors from

Brides Magazine and *Modern Bride*. When representatives from buying offices, bridal boutiques, and department stores made the rounds, I was there to schmooze and walk them through our latest collection. I could charm the most difficult buyer; it was one of my favorite parts of the job.

And then there was the occasional surprise, like when the bridal buyer from Bergdorf's scheduled a meeting with me. A very classy, slightly snooty, grand lady, she was a powerhouse in the New York bridal market. I couldn't believe my luck. What a coup! But she wasn't interested in any of the gowns from my latest collection. Instead, she had a special request.

"We get a lot of girls in here with family veils," she said. "So make me a drop-dead-beautiful, basic dress, a Bergdorf's exclusive that will show off any family heirloom."

Who was I to argue with that? An opportunity to design anything for Bergdorf's didn't come along often, if ever. I did what she asked. I made a long-sleeved, low-back silk satin dress with a bateau neckline and a big bow on the backside with a prominent tail. She liked it so much that she featured it in the store advertisement, and it ended up selling very well. There must have been plenty of brides that year with family heirlooms to wear. I didn't get credit by name or otherwise, but it was an exclusive at Bergdorf's, and that was something to hang my dress on.

Despite the opportunities and successes, I left Bride's World before the year was out. There were issues as there are at any job. Sometimes you have to work with people you don't like, respect, or admire; I knew this from personal experience (remember Josephine?). I also knew I could put up with a lot if it inched me closer to my goals. Every time I sat across the desk from Nate Bernstein, I reminded myself that I finally had my own line.

But in the end, I couldn't stand it. I didn't want to work

for Nate anymore because I didn't trust or like him. I had been down that road more than once; I might even have stayed at Bride's World for another year or two if President Kennedy hadn't been assassinated.

The news of his death broke at lunchtime, when I happened to be out. A big fan of the Kennedys, I was overcome with emotion and disbelief. How could this happen in our country? I returned to work in tears and went straight to Nate's office, where I found him going over paperwork with his assistant. The minute they saw my face, they knew something was up.

"President Kennedy has just been shot in Dallas. Assassinated." I choked out the words. "He's dead."

Nate got up, closed the door to his office, and heaved a long sigh.

"Okay, Victor, take a seat and calm down," he said, fixing me with a sharp look. "I'm going to ask you to not tell anybody else in the office about this. Not yet. We can't afford to have people getting upset and walking out early. There are orders that need to go out by the end of the day, so keep this news to yourself for now."

I think my jaw hit the floor. It was as if everything came into focus, and I saw for the first time what kind of person I was working for. I wanted to quit on the spot; I wanted to yell obscenities at him. I wanted to run into the cutting room and shout that the president of the United States had just been shot dead in Dallas. But in a moment of remarkable self-control, I did none of those things. I nodded, told him I wasn't feeling well, and went home.

For the next few weeks, I avoided Nate as much as possible while planning my next move. I networked, met people for lunch or dinner, dropped hints here and there that a designer I knew was looking for a new job. I'm not a natural liar, but I would have happily told a whopper if it meant I could kiss Bride's World goodbye.

Fortunately, I didn't have to. One evening, Jerry Mantel called me at home, out of the blue, with the news that he had bought out Maria's fifty-percent ownership in Pandora, fired Caroline, and hired a new fitting model. And more, bigger changes were on the way.

"Congratulations, Mr. Mantel," I said. "I'm very happy for you. Why are you calling me about this? I don't work for you anymore."

"I want to change that, Victor," he said. "I want you to be Pandora's lead designer. What will it take?"

"Thirty thousand a year," I said without missing a beat. "I want my own line and thirty thousand. Start there, and then we can talk."

His call may have surprised me, but I'd had plenty of time to think about what I wanted. My answer rolled out fast and easy, with the force of something waiting to be sprung. In 1963, thirty thousand a year was a small fortune for someone like me. I expected him to thank me for my time—or curse me for wasting his—and hang up. There was no way in hell he would agree to pay more than double what I was making at Bride's World. But Mr. Mantel surprised me again.

"I think we can make that work," he said. "Stop by the office next week and we'll iron out the details."

In early 1964, I left Bride's World. Scratch that—I practically ran out the door like my ass was on fire, with Nate insisting that I would regret it. Fat chance.

The move back to Pandora turned out to be a career-changer for me. On my first day as head designer, I announced that we would stage formal shows with professional (or semi-professional) models and seats for buyers and media. No more standing around like commuters waiting for the subway. We would offer a limited number of seats by reservation only. If I was going to be stuck with bridal for a while longer, then I would turn the company into a class act. I would give it cachet.

Over the next several months, I produced shows that rivaled those at Priscilla of Boston and House of Bianchi. Maybe we weren't at their level of fancy—we didn't design Grace Kelly's bridesmaid dresses—but Pandora was hot. I'd like to think it was thanks to me and my new ideas because it probably was. The company received more praise, attention, and magazine covers than ever, and buyers lined up to order from my Victor of Pandora line. I was making good money, and things were going well. Very well. That's usually a sign the other shoe is about to hit the ground.

Sure enough, Terry announced one night that she wanted to move. We had just put the children to bed when she steered me out to the living room and motioned for me to sit down.

"Victor, I'm sick of Brooklyn," she said. "I feel trapped out here, like we're living in exile. I want to move to Manhattan."

"Okay, we'll move to Manhattan," I said.

Some people might have thought I was a pushover for giving in so easily, but I knew the truth: Terry really wanted to move back to Houston. She had made it clear over the past couple of years that she was enduring, not enjoying, life in New York. Houston and Texas were home and always would be. I tried to avoid confrontations around the topic—those never ended well for me. If living in Manhattan would make her happier, then we would move.

We found an apartment on the Upper West Side, a lovely place with a view of Riverside Park. The building was closer to my office on Seventh Avenue. It was also home to lots of families with small children. A perfect place, I thought, for Terry to meet other mothers and start to build a life.

I took that first bridal job in 1959 because I had a wife to support, bills to pay, and a baby on the way—and because no matter how many doors I knocked on or how many sketches I showed, nobody in womenswear would hire me. The bridal industry, on the other hand, welcomed me like a long-lost member of a tight-knit, dysfunctional family. I figured I would design wedding gowns for a year or so, long enough to get some experience and make contacts, and then move on. That was my plan.

You know what they say about plans? First you make them, then life gets in the way. A year came and went. Then another and another. Faster than I could hail a taxi on Broadway, several more years sped by while I built a reputation as one of the better-known bridal designers in New York. I worked in that silk-stocking segment of the fashion world from 1959 to 1965, and during that time I became good at designing all things wedding, from dresses to headpieces and most things in between. Very good. Really, I couldn't complain. By the time I was back at Pandora, I had flocks of customers happy to spend their money on my Victor of Pandora designs. Our reservation-only shows sold out weeks in advance. Editors from the top bridal magazines wined and dined me for exclusives and previews. I should have been celebrating; my success as a bridal designer should have been enough. But after more than six years of coming up with new styles—or new spins on old ones—I was bored. I wanted more. Ironically, thanks to bridal, I got it.

In early 1965, one of my regular buyers stopped by the showroom for a visit. Virginia was a sweet, middle-aged spinster who worked for one of the buying offices. We had a few things in common—mostly our Catholic upbringing and a love of fashion—and we always caught up on gossip and industry news whenever she had an appointment. That particular day, while admiring the beading on one of my latest designs, Virginia asked me if I'd ever thought about moving into womenswear. I couldn't have been more surprised if Grace Kelly had walked through the front door. Had I said something to her about cocktail dresses or suit dresses with a hint of longing in my voice? Could she read my mind? How could she know I'd dreamed of designing clothes for women since middle school? I answered her with an emphatic "Of course!" and confessed that the prospect of being stuck with the title of bridal designer for the rest of my professional days made me want to weep.

"I have a friend who wants to meet you, Victor," she said, patting me on the shoulder. "She's a buyer at Macy's. I told her about your work, and she thinks you would do well in womenswear."

It helped that Virginia was fond of me. I also had a reputation for being even-tempered and easy to work with, rare qualities in the fashion industry back then. That probably hasn't changed much.

"Why don't I make an introduction, and you can take it from there?" she said.

A week later, I found myself in a restaurant in Midtown having lunch with Virginia and her friend, Sherry Simon, from the Little Shop at Macy's.

There was nothing little about Sherry or the shop. It sounded cutesy, but the Little Shop was a big deal in those days, a fancy boutique in Macy's featuring women's designer clothing. Sherry Simon was the boutique's headline buyer. She was also, it turned out, a full-figured, plain-spoken woman who loved to eat and talk. We got on like a burning house.

"Tell me, Victor, do you like what you're doing right now at Pandora?" I liked how she went straight to the point while buttering a roll.

"Well, I'm trained in couture, but the only job I could get when we moved to New York was in bridal," I answered. "I've been doing it for almost seven years."

"Some people I know in bridal think you're hot shit," she said, taking a bite of the roll. "They think you could be doing more than just bridal. I've only seen a few of your dresses, but I can tell you have an eye for what looks good on a woman."

"Thank you, Mrs. Simon," I said. "To me, there's no greater pleasure than making women look and feel beautiful." Maybe it sounded like a bunch of pretentious drivel, but I had drunk my own Kool-Aid. I believed it through and through.

"Call me Sherry." She waved a hand in my direction. "If you're interested in making a move, there's someone I want you to meet."

"I am very interested," I said. "And I would be grateful for any help you can offer."

"Wonderful." She smiled, reaching for another roll. "I'll arrange it."

And just like that, Sherry Simon set up a meeting with the man who would change my life.

Sidney Blauner and his father, Max, were regarded as the closest thing to royalty in the New York garment industry. Together, they owned Lombardy Dress Company, a clothing manufacturer they founded in 1930, along with two other labels: Suzy Perette, known for its affordable copies of ladies' couture designs, and GiGi Young, a source of inexpensive and, in my opinion, cheaply made dresses. With the elder Blauner marching toward retirement, his son decided it was time for Suzy Perette to produce original lines as well as copies of the latest Paris fashions.

That's how I found myself having dinner with Mr. Blauner at Patsy's, an Italian restaurant near Carnegie Hall known for its eclectic clientele of actors, socialites, and mobsters. I arrived at the restaurant a few minutes early. Mr. Blauner showed up half an hour late with a man who looked like the Hollywood version of a Mafia wise guy. Everything about him was dark and off-putting. He wore a charcoal-gray suit, he had dark hair cut short, dark bushy eyebrows, and a nose that looked like it had seen more than a few fights. And he was missing a couple of fingers on his right hand. You didn't see that every day.

I put on my best salesman's smile and tried not to gape at the space where the man's fingers used to be. He seemed like the kind of guy who could dump a body in Long Island Sound and then head to his favorite place for a plate of veal parmigiana. He turned out to be a "business acquaintance" of Mr. Blauner's, though I didn't want to imagine what kind of business they did together. I was relieved when he left after one drink.

Once we were alone, Mr. Blauner laid out his plans. He wanted Suzy Perette to be a company people talked about, one that was taken seriously by the biggest names in high-end retail. To accomplish that, he needed a designer who could share his vision of a grander Suzy Perette. I felt sure that was me.

His son, Richard, who worked in the family business overseeing Jeunesse, a new line featuring clothing for younger women, was supposed to partner with him on this ambitious expansion. But a couple of months earlier, Richard announced he was leaving and taking Jeunesse, with the goal of competing against Suzy Perette. So much for family loyalty. I was sorry for Mr. Blauner and told him so, but one man's defection is another man's opportunity. I wasn't going to waste it.

I assumed we would go home to our families after dinner, think things over, and talk again in a week or two. I never thought he would offer me a job on the spot, but over Bananas Foster and coffee, he told me I was the guy he'd been looking for.

"Why waste time on the dance?" He smiled. "I'm ready to head straight to the altar."

I, on the other hand, approached the situation with more caution than exuberance. I'd been screwed before and I didn't want to find myself in another unhappy mess of a job. Mr. Blauner wasn't looking for a yes-man designer; he wanted a head designer. Me, a head designer at a womenswear manufacturer. The possibility, while thrilling, was also an enormous responsibility, and I wanted to be sure I could handle it. So I offered to use my vacation time for a trial run.

"I don't want anyone to know I'm doing this, Mr. Blauner," I told him. "I haven't quit my job, and I don't plan to yet."

By the end of the two weeks, Mr. Blauner and I would know if we were a good fit. We agreed to keep our arrangement strictly under the table. If things didn't work out, no one would be the wiser and I would have extra cash in the bank.

When I walked into Suzy Perette's offices on 134 West Thirty-Seventh Street, I almost turned around and left. Why would anyone in the fashion industry have offices or showrooms in such a gloomy, dingy building? Designers like Oscar de la Renta and Bill Blass occupied spaces at more elegant addresses two blocks away on Seventh Avenue; Mr. Blauner had four floors in a dungeon. I couldn't imagine buyers traipsing through the dimly lit hallways and showrooms to browse a new collection. On the bright side, the odds of anyone I knew showing up there and recognizing me were negligible. Even so, I was careful to arrive early in the morning and leave after everyone else went home for dinner.

That first week, I reviewed the company's current collections and discovered that the Perette Silhouette, a popular style of cinched-waist, full-skirted dress, was lifted straight from Christian Dior's "New Look" of the 1950s. In fact, most of the company's inventory, old and new, consisted of Dior copies. The biggest difference—the sole difference from what I could tell—was the price tag. Only the very wealthy had money for a tin of Beluga caviar or a Dior original. A Suzy Perette dress, on the other hand, was remarkably affordable. If it looked like a Dior, so much the better.

At the end of the first week, I was halfway through my assessment of the previous season's lookbook when Mr. Blauner came into the office and asked me if I had a passport.

"Of course I do," I said. "I used to live in Paris. Why?"

"Great," he said, rubbing his hands together. "That's where we're going tomorrow night, so why don't you go home early today and make sure you have everything you need for the trip?"

"Mr. Blauner, I'm not your employee," I said. "This is a temporary arrangement, remember?"

"Well, let's make it permanent, and I'll take you to Paris for the spring shows," he said. "We're staying at the Ritz, so quit your job today because this is the last job you're ever going to have."

It felt like a leap into the unknown. I'd never been to the couture shows in Paris, and now I might go as the head designer of a womenswear company. Talk about a brave new world. I have never been one to make rash decisions, but that afternoon, I went to Pandora's offices and quit my job. No two weeks' notice or anything like that. I wasn't leaving on a whim—during my temporary stint at Suzy Perette, Mr. Blauner and I had hashed out my potential salary, title, and responsibilities.

Over dinner that night, I shared the news with Terry that I had accepted a position at Suzy Perette and would be leaving for Paris the next day. I assumed she'd be delighted. It was a good start on my dream come true. Plus it meant more money and less hand-wringing over how we spent every dollar. Our son, Kevin, was nearly six and already in school, and our daughter, Adrienne, would start nursery school in the fall. In a few months, Terry would have time on her hands.

She showered me with congratulations and kisses, but I knew her well enough to know when she was putting on a show. I suppose she pretended for my sake or for the children. Terry couldn't stand living in New York, even though I did everything I could to make things easier for her. I thought maybe if I made more money, bought her nice clothes, or decorated our apartment with French antiques, she would be happier. Instead, the more I made and the more I gave, the more miserable she was. I didn't know what to do. In those days, traditional couples didn't talk about their problems much, if at all; they simply smiled and soldiered on. And we were nothing if not traditional.

I left for Paris the following night with a group of New York fashion industry businessmen that included Mr. Blauner as well as apparel manufacturers Fred Pomerantz of Leslie Fay, Inc., and David Schwartz of Jonathan Logan. Being in the same business doesn't mean you share the same customers. Jonathan Logan was less expensive, Suzy Perette was in the medium price range, and Leslie Fay came in at the higher end with original designs, ladies' suits, and coats. Because they didn't compete directly, they could all be friends, more or less.

Mr. Pomerantz, in particular, was a feisty character who constantly fought with the garment workers' union, saying they were haggling him into the poorhouse. He got so fed up he began using non-union labor in Brooklyn and Staten Island. When the threats came in—presumably from pissed-off union shops—he hired armed guards to ride with his delivery trucks. He wasn't, in his words, "fucking around," and the sooner the union people got the message, the better.

When we landed at Orly Airport the following morning, there was a shiny burgundy Rolls Royce parked on the tarmac. It was the first thing I saw as I stepped out of the plane and started down the stairs. A Rolls Royce, a chauffeur, and, when I turned around, a broad grin on Mr. Pomerantz's face. I shouldn't have been surprised. Apparently, the car was his and he sent it ahead every year by ship with his wife. In fact, he rarely traveled overseas without it. I had been around wealth in Houston, but this kind of extravagance went far beyond anything I'd experienced. I decided right then it was something I could get used to.

Unfortunately, my boss's largesse didn't extend to my accommodations. Given the Rolls Royce welcome at the airport, I thought my room at the Ritz might have a view of the Place Vendôme. No such luck. The *chambre de bonne* I squeezed myself and my suitcase into had a partial view of the alley behind the hotel. Yes, it was a shoebox of a room, but at least it was in the Ritz. That night, I dreamed of how Terry and I shared crepes at a stand in the Latin Quarter the day after our wedding. Even in my dream, it felt like a lifetime and a half ago, as if those two people were strangers.

That first trip to the Paris shows was an eye-opener. Mr. Blauner invited a different group of buyers and fashion writers to join us every night for dinner. It was good business and, since Mr. Blauner also liked to eat well, good food. I usually came down to the lobby early to indulge in people-watching. Few places are better for observing the comings and goings of the beautiful and the well-to-do than the lobby of an exclusive hotel.

One night, while I was waiting for Mr. Blauner, I spotted Barbara "Babe" Paley emerging from the elevator in a striking couture frock, trailed by her two daughters, no doubt off to a post-show dinner at Lasserre or La Tour d'Argent. Mrs. Paley was *quelque chose* in those days. Cosmopolitan socialite, perennial icon on the best-dressed lists, and wife of CBS founder William S. Paley, she regularly appeared in gossip columns and style pages from New York to Los Angeles. I was admiring her Balenciaga outfit when she walked up to me.

"Hello there, we've seen you here every night this week," she said, giving me an appraising look. "What are you doing in Paris?"

"Well, my name is Victor Costa." I stood up, flustered. "I'm going to be a designer, and I love your Balenciaga."

It made me sound ingenuous, like a character from *It's a Wonderful Life*, but it was the truth, wasn't it? I was there as a designer, and I planned to design the hell out of a new Suzy Perette line after this trip. Mrs. Paley smiled at me, practically patting me on the head as if I were a little boy.

"It is a good one, isn't it?" she said, glancing down the length of her skirt as if to confirm that, yes, it was a spectacular outfit. "I'm Mrs. Paley. Nice to meet you, Mr. Costa. Have a lovely evening and best of luck with your designs." With a wave, she and her daughters swept out the door so quickly I didn't have a chance to say thank you.

Mr. and Mrs. Blauner materialized next to me, and we watched Mrs. Paley's limousine drive off into the drizzly Paris night.

"What are we waiting for? Let's go, or we'll be late for our reservation." He hustled us toward the line of taxis. "Who was that? I was too far away to see."

"Nobody special," I said, smiling to myself. "Just another lady with fabulous taste and money to spend."

We arrived at the restaurant a little damp but on time. Mr. Blauner always dined at the finest, most see-and-be-seen places whenever he traveled, and this one was no different: tasteful, warmly lit, and full of manicured, well-dressed men and women. As I sat down between the two Blauners, the missus leaned over me, giving her husband a sly look.

"Sidney, you're never going to believe who's sitting at the next table," she whispered. "Babe Paley. The Babe Paley."

"No kidding!" he said. "Which one is she?"

He turned around in his chair and half stood up, head swiveling back and forth for a better view. I focused on the menu in front of me.

"You have the subtlety of a bull moose, Sidney," Mrs. Blauner sighed. "She's wearing the fur-trimmed dress, and she's just as elegant as her pictures."

I lowered my menu in time to see Mr. Blauner zero in on Mrs. Paley, recognize her as the woman from the Ritz, and then turn back to me, eyes narrowed. I gave a little shrug, as if to say, *I know more than you think I do*, and reached for my water. Now he knew, too.

CHAPTER 11

Everyone talks about how location is what matters most in real estate. In 1965, it also mattered in fashion, and, after that first Paris trip, it was obvious that Suzy Perette's showroom was in a wholly undesirable spot. The company had four floors in a shabby old building on West Thirty-Seventh Street, where the designing, cutting, sewing, and showings happened. There were legitimate retail buyers who came to browse and order from our collections, and there were shoppers and some retail buyers who headed straight to the second floor, where we kept a sizable inventory of leftover dresses hanging on pipe racks.

Some models were from the previous season, and some were current but not selling well. If you liked Suzy Perette's clothes and knew about the secret stash, you'd go to the second floor, choose your favorites, and buy them at a discount—as long as you paid in cash. I never did ask Mr. Blauner whether his booming side business skirted the law or broke it; I didn't care. Neither did the buyers who paid for last season's leftovers with brown paper bags full of cash. But some buyers—those who stocked their departments with our higher-end designs from season to season—did care.

"Mr. Blauner, I've heard our retail customers don't like coming here," I said to him one afternoon. "They like our clothes, but they'd rather shop in a nicer space."

"Well, nobody has said anything about it before," he snorted.

"Yes, but that was then," I said. "Now we need to offer

them something new, improved, and more convenient."

As a buyer, why would you walk a few blocks to see one line of clothing when you could see ten different lines in one place? There were two buildings on Seventh Avenue where most of the popular designers and manufacturers had showrooms. If Mr. Blauner wanted to court the big-name retailers, he needed to step up his game. It took a couple of months of looking and negotiating before I found a showroom at 498 Seventh Avenue, one of the two coveted locations.

I'd like to say that I single-handedly convinced him to sign the lease, but the truth is less heroic. My boss was, above all, a businessman, so it must have made sense to spend some money in order to make more. We hired a designer to refurbish the space, dressing it up with tufted leather sofas, glass coffee tables, and plenty of lighting to make the clothes and the ladies look their best. It was like we'd moved to a different planet, not around the corner. And nobody was more excited about the new showroom than Suzy Perette's publicist, Eleanor Lambert.

First, let me say that Eleanor Lambert, known as the Empress of Seventh Avenue, was a genius, a visionary, an influencer in the age of print publications, broadcast television, and rotary-dial phones. This woman, who wore Lilly Daché hats and turbans to hide her unfortunate, straggly blonde hair, had the New York fashion industry and media eating out of her hand. Her performance as a fashion publicist notwithstanding, she racked up a long list of accomplishments that included founding the Met Gala, the International Best Dressed List, the Council of Fashion Designers of America, and New York Press Week (which became Fashion Week). By the time I met her, she was already a legend. I couldn't imagine what she had left to do. Run her business? Expand her network of media contacts? Find a new hairdresser? Make me famous?

Apparently, Mr. Blauner and Eleanor were conspiring to

get my name out among buyers, shoppers, and fashionistas and, in the process, strike gold for Suzy Perette. Of course, I had no clue what they were up to, and that probably kept me from collapsing under the weight of their expectations. The campaign to make me famous began with my first Press Week show.

Press Week, or what we now call New York Fashion Week, started as a showcase for established and emerging New York fashion designers. If you were Eleanor's client, she selected items from a current line, had pictures taken, wrote up a bio about the designer, and put all these elements together as a display in your showroom. She called it Press Week because it was her idea and she could call it whatever she wanted, but also because she invited members of the press from New York and across the country to come and see what fashion designers in New York were up to. She hosted breakfasts, lunches, and dinners for editors and writers because they needed something to feature in their style pages, and Press Week was a land of discovery.

Here's how it worked. I got the same one-hour slot as well-known names like Kasper, Geoffrey Beene, and Bill Blass. In that time, we showed samples from our latest collections and hoped that reporters requested photos and information. They could write a story, but they couldn't run it until Eleanor released the photos for publication.

My first Press Week did, in fact, turn out to be a career-making moment, but not because reporters hailed me as the designer *du jour*. More than a few liked my designs enough to write about them, and buyers ordered my designs en masse, leading Eleanor to declare my official debut a great success. In many ways, her opinion mattered more than Mr. Blauner's. He signed my paycheck, but she pulled the levers of power, made things happen, and got people to pay attention. Eleanor was a fashion kingmaker; it meant something to bask in the glow of her approval. But that's not why Press Week of 1965 proved so critical to my future as a designer. Much of the credit for that goes to a woman named Sarah.

Sarah was the womenswear buyer at De Pinna, a clothing store that was, at the time, a distinguished member of New York's retail world. She may not have been a reporter or an editor, but Sarah hit all the shows during Press Week, and she had a remarkable knack for discovering trends, new fashions, and new designers. When she asked me if I wanted to join her for the launch of a new collection from a designer named Oscar de la Renta, I said yes. Her enthusiasm was enough to pique my curiosity.

Oscar had a résumé to envy: stints in couture at Balenciaga, Dior, and Lanvin, and in ready-to-wear at Elizabeth Arden in New York. His most recent gig at Jane Derby found him suddenly in charge of the design house when Jane herself died unexpectedly in Bermuda. His first solo show opened under the new label of Oscar de la Renta for Jane Derby.

"Victor, you're going to love his work," Sarah gushed over the phone. "It's vibrant and gorgeous. He's going to be big. I can feel it."

How could anyone say no to that? So I went to the show and left bedazzled by the dresses, the fabrics, the fairy-tale mood evoked by his clothes. I didn't need a crystal ball to predict his success or my lifelong love affair with his clothes. I could see the direction he was moving in, the colors and shapes, the romance and beauty—it made me want to create a new Suzy Perette line based on his designs. But when I proposed a series of long dresses, Mr. Blauner shut me down.

"Nobody will wear long dresses," he said. Never mind that I'd just seen a show where eveningwear was the main attraction.

We remained at an uncomfortable impasse until Eleanor came up with the idea for me to design and make long dresses for six of the current season's debutantes. Young ladies making their formal entry into society may seem like a quaint, obsolete tradition in the age of crypto billionaires and dating apps, but it has endured as a rite of passage for women of a certain social pedigree. Back then, it was de *rigueur* among New York's bluebloods, and Eleanor knew how to make the most of it. She wanted to photograph the debutantes in my dresses for a full-page, full-color spread in the *New York Herald Tribune*. Her friend, Eugenia Sheppard, the newspaper's fashion columnist, offered to write a companion piece about high society and haute design.

"Think of the publicity, Sidney," Eleanor said. "This could be a great opportunity for Suzy Perette."

"No, absolutely not. I don't want our name on those dresses," Mr. Blauner said. "Nobody will wear them." For someone who had spent decades working in the fashion industry, he could be short-sighted.

"Then why don't we make it a new line and call it Romantica by Victor Costa?" Eleanor said. The woman was stupendous and scary; it was as if she stockpiled creative contingency plans for every situation. "Without your label, people won't associate it with Suzy Perette," she continued. "But I'm telling you, Sidney, women will buy these dresses. I promise you, they will sell."

And then you'll be sorry—I didn't say it out loud, but the possibility of those words drifted between us like a cloying floral perfume. In the end, she wore him down with an answer for every objection until he agreed, as long as Suzy Perette's name was nowhere to be seen. Thanks to Eleanor Lambert, Mr. Blauner got what he wanted, and I got my first womenswear line.

I worked days, nights, and weekends. I stayed late at the office and worked when I went home. To my family, I was a ghost. I left for the office before the children were up and came home in the dark, after dinner and the nightly bedtime story; I missed important occasions and school events. My constant absence became a sore spot with Terry, who showed up at the door every night with a fresh cocktail and a litany of complaints. It was a side of her I hadn't seen before. I explained that my grueling schedule was temporary. With Eleanor breathing down my neck, insisting that every dress had to be extraordinary, work had to come before family. This was my big chance—I didn't want to screw it up. I didn't really have a choice, did I?

"You're right, I am working this hard to get ahead in my career," I said after an especially nasty exchange during which Terry accused me of being selfish and too ambitious. "But I'm also doing this for us, so we can have a better life."

She didn't always buy that argument, even though it was at least half true. I did want to give my wife and children the best of everything, even if I had to work my knuckles to the bone. But I'd have been lying if I didn't admit that I craved professional success, recognition, and acceptance, sometimes more than anything. I did what I could to defuse a fight with Terry; when she was too far gone in anger, I learned to ignore her.

Do you know what came out of that collection, aside from my initial taste of fame? My first official crumb catcher dress. Originally designed to be a costume for the theater, the crumb catcher featured a pleated or ruffled bodice that stood up and slightly away from a woman's chest. The idea was that it could catch any stray crumbs because the last thing a well-bred lady wanted was a sprinkling of crumbs across her front or down her skirt. The crumb catcher also hinted at a gorgeous bosom. It made men want to peek at—or imagine—the glories that lay beneath those ruffles.

The original Romantica by Victor Costa crumb catcher was cut from a beautiful aqua chiffon with a wide, olive-green satin band around the waist. The bodice bloomed upward; the skirt rippled and flowed as if caught in a breeze. It was a spectacular dress! So was the rest of that collection. When the *Herald Tribune* published the article with a picture of the debutantes in my designs, buyers went crazy. The dresses sold out, buyers ordered more, and those sold out, too. As I'd predicted, women wanted pretty, feminine evening wear—and Romantica by Victor Costa gave it to them. In two years, my line would account for half of Suzy Perette's annual sales. Not bad for a style of dress nobody wanted to wear.

Mr. Blauner never admitted he was wrong about the dresses. A thank-you would have been nice, but he wasn't good at showing shame or gratitude. He didn't take bad news well, either. In one meeting, he threw a pair of scissors at the head of production because he didn't like what the poor man was telling him. Yes, Mr. Blauner was a bit of a tyrant, but he gave me a job and the freedom to move my ideas from the sketch pad to the cutting room to the showroom. Who else was confident or fool enough to take that gamble?

A few weeks after the launch of my line, he told me I had an appointment with the company attorney that afternoon at three o'clock. I don't know why I didn't ask about the reason for the appointment—chalk it up to distraction or inexperience—but I showed up on time and sat down with the lawyer, who handed me some forms to sign. One of the many things I learned from my mother was to read everything before I signed anything, so I took my time and pored over every page, including the fine print. If I signed those forms, I would be signing away the right to use my name on my designs. Mr. Blauner made me famous, and now he wanted to own my name. He must have realized his mistake in letting me have a line that, on the surface, had no association with Suzy Perette, especially as the dresses continued to sell out. I left that meeting, more disappointed than angry, without signing the forms.

In 1966, a year after I started working at Suzy Perette, I was invited to join the Council of Fashion Designers of America. I wouldn't say I was awestruck, but it was quite an honor for an up-and-comer like me to be rubbing elbows with some of the country's best-known designers. I met Bill Blass at the first meeting I attended. His womenswear collections for Maurice Rentner Ltd. had a large and devoted following. A little star-struck, I walked over and introduced myself.

"Hello Mr. Blass, I'm Victor Costa from Suzy Perette," I said.

"No, you are Victor Costa," he said. "Don't ever do that. Don't ever give publicity to anyone but yourself."

Given that my boss had asked me to sign away my name, it seemed like excellent advice. I took it and never looked back.

CHAPTER 12

Mr. Blauner and I traveled to Paris twice a year for business. We went for the couture shows, for the meetings with important buyers and fashion editors, and for a shot of French culture and cuisine. But above all, we went to acquire and copy other designers' clothes.

Every store in the U.S. worth shopping at had some Paris copies. This was around the same time Yves Saint Laurent unveiled his first ready-to-wear line at his Rive Gauche boutique in Paris, upending the fashion world yet again. Designer clothes—not made-to-order couture—at a lower price point was a concept that would eventually enjoy great success in the U.S. and around the world, but in 1966 stores still depended on "line for line promotions," or near-perfect copies of couture designs. It was all above board. In fact, line for line promotions were done with the blessing and cooperation of the couture houses. They wanted to make money as much as we did, and the U.S. was a very big market full of shoppers eager to wear a Dior or Chanel knock-off. For everyone involved, it was about the bottom line.

I trained to make straight, exact copies during my year at design school in Paris; it was part of the classwork. When I joined Suzy Perette, I put the skills I learned as a student to work as a designer. But we didn't wander in for a look at Givenchy's latest creations and take photos. Clothing manufacturers like Leslie Fay and Suzy Perette had to pay a "caution," or a fee, to get into the shows. A caution, which could run into the tens of thousands of dollars, bought you a pleasant afternoon in a couture showroom along with a couple of toiles, first drafts of a garment made from cheap linen or cotton fabric. If you wanted the original, that was extra.

Of course, we never settled for toiles. Mr. Blauner refused to walk out the door without a couple of originals in hand because purchasing the originals also gave him the right to use the designer's name. To be able to say "This is a Dior copy," "This is a Balenciaga copy," "This is a Chanel copy," and so on was a selling point, and we wanted every point we could get. But the caution, whether it was ten thousand dollars or twenty thousand, gave you the right to duplicate a certain number of dresses, usually two or three. You can imagine how many fabulous designs were featured in any given show—were we really supposed to limit ourselves to a pair? Thanks to my talent for recall, we didn't have to.

Mr. Blauner and I always took our time browsing a new collection. What was the point of speed-walking through a Saint Laurent show, after all? Whenever he saw a garment he thought would sell well, Mr. Blauner nudged me, a sign that I should linger in front of that particular model, memorize the details, colors, and cut. Once we paid for our originals and left the building, I would go back to the hotel and sketch the other pieces he wanted. Ten or fifteen or twenty for the price of two was a much better deal.

Together, Mr. Blauner and I usually arrived in Paris with about two hundred and fifty thousand dollars to spend. It was a shocking amount of money to have on hand, but we left with thirty or so original couture dresses and another three hundred in my sketch pad—all our ideas for the next six months. That investment paid for itself. In those days, there were no bloggers snapping shots with smartphones; there was no instant notification, no social media or posting of pictures within hours of a big reveal. Only those who attended a Dior show knew the splendors of the new line because the design houses controlled everything, from when photos were released to the press to when the press was allowed to publish them.

No trip to the Paris shows was complete without lots of wining and dining. Manufacturers like Suzy Perette had to be friendly with the press to get coverage and with stores to get and keep their business, so we held court at the Ritz. Breakfast on Sunday morning for a dozen guests. An elegant lunch with fashion writers like Bernadine Morris of the *New York Times* and Eugenia Sheppard from the *International Herald Tribune*. Dinner with the fashion directors of stores that did line for line promotions like Saks Fifth Avenue, Orbach's, Ellis Ayres, and J.L. Hudson. We charmed and schmoozed and cut deals over omelets and croissants, escargot and coq au vin and glasses of full-bodied Cabernet. There were certainly worse ways to do business.

Despite the outrage in some designer circles, there was nothing officially wrong with copying designs that weren't part of the line for line deal. Not then and not now. Some may consider it unacceptable, unethical, even a little sneaky, but it's not illegal because clothing is practical—it keeps us from walking around naked—unlike a novel or a song, which in the eyes of the courts aren't necessities and therefore protected by copyrights. That said, when line for line was the norm, ladies flocked to the stores as soon as the latest Paris copies showed up. And it wasn't because they were in the mood for something practical to wear.

Don't get me wrong. Couture designs weren't extravagantly wacky as some are today; they didn't make strong statements, except to draw attention to their beauty or cheekiness. There was no Lacroix. No Mugler. No McQueen or McCartney. We had Givenchy, Pierre Cardin, Balenciaga, Chanel, Courrèges, and a few others. I remember during one of our shopping trips, Mr. Blauner and I went to the Chanel showroom. I don't know what I expected—something different, something updated, classy or exciting—but it wasn't happening at Chanel.

"What do you think of these?" Mr. Blauner asked me as we examined cocktail and evening dresses as well as a handful of the trademark suits.

"To be honest, I don't think we want to make clothes for old ladies," I said, pointing to a tweed outfit. "My mother wouldn't be caught dead wearing this." That was before Karl Lagerfeld took over the label in the 1980s and transformed it.

Dior was another couture house whose popularity I didn't understand. Call me a contrarian, but with Marc Bohan in charge, Dior made some of the most basic, uninspired pieces I've ever seen. I mean, this was Dior of the New Look, Dior who put the feminine back in women's clothing. Bohan's designs should have knocked the breath right out of me; instead, they put me to sleep. Yves Saint Laurent, on the other hand, managed to create sophisticated clothes that were also inventive in their way, especially after he left Dior and started his own label. I loved copying his designs, and women couldn't wait to buy them.

You might think French couturiers took a dim view of the mass merchandising of their designs to American women. Some certainly did. But many understood that line for line copies and the U.S. market were important pieces of their business. As much as fashion design is about art and creativity, it's also about making money. At the end of the day, if you make clothes that don't sell, no matter how magnificent they are, you're going out of business. So they put up with line for line; some even encouraged it. It was good for everyone, designers and copycats alike, until Saint Laurent launched the Rive Gauche ready-to-wear line in the fall of 1966 and began selling it in his Paris boutique. After that, it was just a matter of time (and survival) before other important designers embraced ready-to-wear.

Saint Laurent was the first to make his designs available

off the rack and at lower prices. It was a bold move designed to appeal to a younger generation as well as women who didn't have the money for couture (which was almost everyone). The truth was that even those less expensive outfits and separates remained out of reach for most shoppers. My copies, on the other hand, were an affordable splurge. A Rive Gauche dress might cost one hundred fifty dollars (remember, this was the 1960s), while a Suzy Perette version of the same dress might sell for seventy-five dollars. Which one do you think a house-wife from Indianapolis was more likely to buy? I was betting on the copies.

It was at a Saint Laurent show in 1967 that Dame Margot Fonteyn helped me choose one of our biggest sellers. Mr. Blauner had broken his leg and couldn't travel, so I went to Paris without him. Not only did I have to navigate the Paris shows solo with tens of thousands of dollars in cash in my briefcase, but I also had to decide which samples to purchase and which to copy. It wasn't as if I could take a few pictures and text them to Mr. Blauner for his opinion. The responsibility for choosing wisely was mine alone.

A couple of days into jet lag, I went to the Saint Laurent show and found a front-row seat—the closer the better for remembering details like buttons, beading, embroidery, and fabric. With the pre-show schmoozing in high gear, I didn't notice when a couple claimed the two seats on my left. It took me a few beats to realize they were, in fact, the great prima ballerina Dame Margot Fonteyn and her friend and dance partner Rudolf Nureyev. I'm not easily starstruck, but I'll admit I was a little dazzled to be sitting next to two of the most celebrated ballet dancers of the twentieth century. Was I supposed to make polite conversation or leave them alone? Smile or look away? Or both? Dame Margot came to my rescue, introducing herself and Mr. Nureyev and then peppering me with questions about what I did and why I was at the show. In a gracious, elegant way, of course.

"My name is Victor Costa," I told her. "I'm a designer for an American company and, to be honest, I'm here because my boss couldn't make it. I have to find something that will sell well in the U.S."

"Well, Victor, why don't we see what Monsieur Saint Laurent has to offer today?" She smiled, patting my arm. "I feel confident you'll find something."

We sat and watched the models emerge from behind the curtain in coats, eveningwear, dresses, blouses, and skirts as I waited for something to jump out at me. I have been a Saint Laurent devotee for decades, but that day the thrill eluded me; I dreaded the prospect of going home without at least a piece or two to copy. An hour into the show, I was ready to call it quits when Dame Margot tapped me on the shoulder and nodded toward the catwalk, as if to say, *That one*. The model wore a striped shirtdress—on the surface, a dress like many others, except that it wasn't. The neckline sported a pussycat bow, and the knee-length skirt had stitched-down pleats so it fluttered when she walked. It was breezy and sophisticated, and it looked like something women would love to wear.

What did I have to lose? Since the press wasn't allowed to release any photographs of the collection for a month, I could get the dress made and shipped out before newspapers and magazines published pictures of the original. I had already paid the caution, so I took the sample with me and headed back to New York. I assumed Mr. Blauner would congratulate me for choosing this Dame Margot-approved Saint Laurent. Instead, he turned purple with fury. For a minute, I thought he might throw one of his crutches at me.

"Are you fucking crazy?" he bellowed. "I send you to Paris, and you come back with a shirtdress?"

"Mr. Blauner, give me a chance to show you why I chose this dress," I said to him. "It's going to be a big hit. I think women will sprint to the stores to buy it."

For a minute, I thought about telling him that Dame Margot

Fonteyn had actually spotted the dress first. Then, knowing how he might react to that bit of information, I decided to keep my mouth shut. What Mr. Blauner didn't know couldn't hurt me. Probably.

I had a feeling my job might be on the line with this dress, so I called my friend Kal Ruttenstein, who was then the buyer at the Town Shop in Lord & Taylor. One of the most interesting characters I've ever known, Kal had impeccable taste, a near-perfect record for predicting fashion trends, and an insatiable appetite for good food, young men, and fine art. We often had dinner together to talk about work, industry gossip, or the latest exhibit at the Metropolitan; more often than not, when I arrived to pick him up I'd run into a handsome young man (or two) coming out the front door, a sheepish smile on his face.

The steady stream of twenty-somethings drifting in and out of his apartment never failed to surprise me. Not because Kal was gay—I couldn't have cared less whom or how many he invited into his bed—but because he was paunchy, balding, and always on some kind of fad diet. He had brains and wit, not beauty. Maybe those young men were high-rent help. Maybe they were models or aspiring designers hoping that a tit for tat with Kal would advance their careers. Or maybe, like me, they simply enjoyed his company. In any case, I had to prove to Mr. Blauner that buying the striped dress with the pussycat bow was a smart decision, and I knew Kal could help me sell it.

The Town Shop at Lord & Taylor featured only daytime wear. I cut a deal with Kal: if the dress sold as well as I hoped it would, I would give the Town Shop an exclusive. I found some cheap blue-and-white-striped fabric—it had to be inexpensive because of the stitched-down pleats and full skirt—cut the pattern, and made the dress. The first batch we sent over to the Town Shop flew off the rack, so we made more. And when those sold, we made even more. In the end, we sold more than ten thousand, an impressive number by any measure.

"Mr. Blauner, you ranted and railed about this dress. You said I was crazy, that nobody would buy it," I said to him after the last shipment left the warehouse. "I want to point out that we have cut ten thousand of the dress nobody wanted. Where is your apology?"

Of course, there wasn't one. Sidney Blauner never admitted he was wrong about much of anything—and certainly not about the shirtdress with the pussycat bow. But he didn't question my judgment again.

I knew my copies could fool even the most experienced eye, but I had a chance to prove it one afternoon when Mildred Custin stopped by the showroom. The legendary president of Bonwit Teller, Mrs. Custin was famous for, among other things, bringing Pierre Cardin for men to that upscale women's store. Mr. Blauner invited her to come by and browse our latest selection of Dior copies.

She wasn't there five minutes when she mentioned a certain floor-length dress that grabbed her attention in Paris; was there any chance we copied it? Of course. I also had the original Dior sample and offered to show her both. I dressed one live model in my copy and another in the original and sent them out together without identifying which was which. When I joined her a few minutes later, she stood in front of the two models, shaking her head.

"Victor, look at your bow," she said, pointing to the dress on the left. "And the hem and collar don't look right compared to the Dior." She waved a hand at the other dress. "Now *that* is an example of fine craftsmanship and design. You can do better."

"Mrs. Custin, please look at the labels," I laughed. "You're taking issue with the Dior. The dress on the right is mine."

I really was that good. Probably because I worked all the time. Sure, I had a discerning eye, I was creative, and I could make a pattern, but people who knew me said I didn't know when to stop working. They were right. And honestly, I think the constant work helped me become one of the best fashion copyists, if not *the* best, in the industry. Even when I started working for Mr. Blauner, I kept a side gig designing wedding gowns and bridesmaid dresses for Contessa, a bridal company. I figured if things went south for me at Suzy Perette, I would have some kind of income to fall back on.

There was just one issue: I didn't want Mr. Blauner to find out about my moonlighting. Instead of accepting money from Contessa, I asked for payment in services or goods. A new sofa or coffee table. Carpentry work or painting. It came down to tit for tat—*If I do this for you, what can you do for me?*—which is how Terry and I came to have our apartment decorated.

When the people at Contessa asked me to design a wedding dress for one of their clients—an editor at *Women's Wear Daily*—I agreed to do it. In exchange, I wanted the editor's mother, a well-known interior decorator, to overhaul our new apartment on Riverside Drive. I made a magical gown with the finest *gros de Londres* silk, the decorator did a fabulous job pulling together our apartment with new fabrics, curtains, and furniture, and Contessa paid the bills. It wasn't cash in the bank, but it was one way to get things done.

Don't get me wrong. I made good money at my job, but I was worth more than Mr. Blauner paid me. My daily grind began early in the morning and didn't end until after Terry and the children went to bed. I designed, negotiated, argued, purchased, shopped, brainstormed, cut, and sewed. I hardly had a minute for my family or myself, but I never turned down the extra work. And when summer rolled around, my work schedule took over my life completely. As soon as school was over, Terry packed up the kids and fled to Houston. For three months, she had two sets of grandparent babysitters and an abundance of free time to do whatever she wanted. Who knows what she got up to down there—I sure didn't—but she never thought twice about going. It was clear she didn't mind leaving me on my own for the entire summer.

Not that I was alone very often. With my family away and me living a bachelor's life, Mr. Blauner figured he owned me and my time, weekends included. Every Saturday, he and Giulietta, a bosomy Italian girl who worked as our fitting model, picked me up in his chauffeur-driven Rolls Royce. Anyone else would have thought it odd that they always showed up together, Giulietta smiling and rosy as a new bride, but I had already heard that when it came to women, Mr. Blauner had a wandering eye. Nothing surprised me then or now, but I did wonder how Mrs. Blauner felt about her husband's taste for other women.

I also asked myself how my wife could leave me alone for three months. Did she think about what I might be doing during my bachelor summers? After all, I had needs; didn't she have them, too? I wasn't a womanizer. I took our marriage vows seriously, and Terry knew that. As Catholics, we lived by the rules, whether or not we agreed with them. We didn't have a picture-perfect marriage, far from it, but we had two kids and, at some point in our shared history, we loved each other. At that moment, that was reason enough to stay together.

Mr. Blauner, Giulietta, and I spent many Saturdays reconnoitering at Macy's, B. Altman, Lord & Taylor, Bonwit Teller, Saks Fifth Avenue, and Bloomingdale's, shopping for what was new and what we could copy. Giulietta tried on different dresses and outfits at every store, but we didn't buy anything. At the time, when you were shopping to copy, someone else—not the copyist or the fitting model—usually purchased the clothes and then returned them in a day or two. That was the industry norm, probably because copyists didn't want designers and their contacts in high-end retail stores to know which dresses or suits they were going to copy. Mr. Blauner and I would discuss which designs we thought would do well in the Suzy Perette line, and, on Monday morning, I would tell the three young women who shopped for us where to go and what to buy. Off they'd go, cash in hand.

If there were three pieces from Geoffrey Beene featured in the window at Bonwit's, one of our shoppers would buy two pieces and another would buy the third. One young woman buying all three outfits might be a red flag, since everyone in the fashion world knew I regularly copied his designs. It wasn't as if we were doing anything illegal; it was more an issue of keeping up appearances. I didn't want Geoffrey Beene or any other designer to know what I was up to ahead of time; I preferred to keep things quiet until my copies were let loose in the world.

We sent shoppers out to buy what we had scouted. They hit stores for dresses by lots of designers; among my favorites were Oscar de la Renta and Dior, whose fashions were, easy to copy and sold very well. At the end of the day, each of them came back with an armful of garments. After Giulietta tried everything on, I told our patternmakers—a mother, son, and daughter from China—to make it like this or that, or to not change a thing. They worked nonstop, all day and night copying, cutting, and sewing, so the next day we had new finished pieces for the Suzy Perette line. Once they were done, the shoppers returned every outfit or dress they'd bought. We ran a very efficient operation.

With my copies, you couldn't say "This is the Geoffrey Beene, and this is the Victor Costa copy." After all, I fooled Mildred Custin, didn't I? If you placed the original and the copy side by side, they looked almost identical. Of course, there were always a few differences here and there. If a dress was made from a heavy wool, I changed the fabric. If the brocade on an outfit was too pricey, I substituted something less expensive to make it pretty. Because I could remember and recreate everything about a garment down to the stitch on a hem, I would have been stupid not to channel that ability into copying beautiful clothes. And nobody has ever accused me of being stupid. Naïve, yes, but not stupid.

My naïveté was on full display the day Mr. Blauner asked me to take a fashion model to lunch. Not a Sears catalog model but an "It" girl. This young woman was a supermodel in the late 1960s, before the term even existed. She moved through a room with feline elegance, exuding sexiness and confidence, thrilling qualities in a model—really, in any woman. I met her when she was on the cusp of becoming a household name.

I had recently finished a new line of dresses, and Eleanor Lambert wanted pictures of them. Press Week wasn't for a couple of months, but Eleanor was nothing if not organized. She even had a model in mind.

"There's a girl I want to use for Victor's press pictures," she told Mr. Blauner during a phone call. "She's back from a fashion shoot in Africa. I'm sending her over to you tomorrow, so be charming."

Mr. Blauner could charm high-level department store executives and couture designers, but it didn't come naturally to him. In fact, he didn't like socializing, talking on the phone, or making nice with models; he usually dumped that work on me. So when this leggy, tan, blonde beauty with a hint of a Southern drawl walked into the showroom, he assigned me the task of entertaining her. It was just as well. Not five minutes after she arrived, she gave Mr. Blauner a big, toothy grin and pointed out that his nose hairs needed a trim. She was right. He had a full head of hair sprouting inside his nose, but what was the point of making it public? She laughed as if she'd said something hilarious and asked to look at the new line. No wonder he didn't like models.

"Victor, why don't you take our guest to lunch and then come back for fittings?" Mr. Blauner said through gritted teeth.

I got the hint and whisked her downstairs to a very good, very pricey restaurant where we often entertained editors, buyers, and special clients.

"Eleanor told me that you recently spent time on a shoot in Africa," I said after we ordered. "I've never been. What was it like?"

"Hot," she said, flashing a slightly crooked smile.

As she spoke, I felt something under the table stroking my leg. Her foot. There wasn't much of an age difference between us—she was in her mid-twenties, I was in my early thirties—but she was bold, confident, a little intimidating. And she had quite a foot.

"I've heard it can be very hot," I said, trying to ignore what was happening under the table. "Where did you go?"

"Kenya," she said. "Do you want to fuck?"

Yes, the supermodel-to-be asked me to have sex, right there, before the salads arrived, as if she were casually reaching for a roll and a pat of butter. Maybe she fucked men she didn't know all the time, or maybe she was horny right then and I was conveniently at the same table. I didn't care why; I was shocked and, to be honest, a little aroused. I told her I was married, which elicited a husky chuckle, politely turned down her offer, and made it through lunch without choking.

That wasn't the first time I'd been propositioned, but it was among the most memorable. I always turned them down, sometimes, I admit, with regret. With Terry away for the entire summer, I found myself increasingly longing for physical and emotional intimacy. Work helped to fill some, but not all, of the emptiness. And while I usually succeeded in not feeling too sorry for myself, it wasn't easy. One day, a friend set something altogether different in motion. Bill McCall was fashion director at Lord & Taylor when Kal Ruttenstein was the buyer at the Town Shop. Like Kal, Bill was overtly homosexual, a little unconventional, and all sorts of fun. As Lord & Taylor was one of Suzy Perette's best customers, he and I often met to talk business and, occasionally, we would have lunch. During one of those meetings about a window display featuring my newest dresses, Bill stopped mid-conversation and looked me up and down.

"Have you ever been to bed with a man?" he said.

I was flabbergasted. Such a scandalous and intimate question pulled out of thin air.

"Of course not," I snapped, a small rumble of outrage—or was it nerves? —rolling through me. "I'm a married man, and I'm not homosexual." I could have mentioned that I stuck to my vows even when facing down a gorgeous, horny model, but I figured Bill wouldn't care.

"Fine, you're married." He waved a hand at me. "But have you ever had sex with a man?"

"Don't be ridiculous," I said, suddenly not sure whether to be offended or intrigued. Or both.

"Well, I'll take care of that," he said. Because he, like everyone else I worked or socialized with, knew that my wife and children moved to Texas for the summer and I was home alone in our apartment on Riverside Drive. Apparently being a sucker for cocktail dresses and anything designed by Jacques Fath also meant that my sexual preferences might be flexible. Why did a man have to be a homosexual to appreciate women's clothing?

"What are you talking about?" I said. "This is a silly conversation. Let's focus on deciding which dresses you want for the front windows."

That night, I didn't get home until dinnertime. I was tired, overworked, and planning for a business trip to Ohio the next day. Somewhere in the back of my mind, I was also musing, a little uncomfortably, about Bill's inappropriate suggestion. When the doorman called to tell me that someone had dropped off a package, I didn't think anything of it.

"Send it up, please, Johnny," I said, distracted by my thoughts.

A few minutes later, I opened the door to find an attractive, red-haired young man in his mid-twenties standing in my hallway. I recognized him as one of the window dressers at Lord & Taylor.

"Did Bill make you come all the way up here to drop something off?" I said, looking for a package or an envelope and seeing none. "The doorman said you had a package."

The redhead leaned toward me. "I am the package," he whispered. "Special delivery." He walked past me into my apartment, while I stood there gaping.

Shock notwithstanding, I knew what I was doing when I closed the door. A few hours later, I could no longer say I'd never had sex with a man, nor could I say I didn't enjoy it. I did, and I left for Cleveland the next morning as scheduled, burdened with equal amounts of guilt and satisfaction. A day and a half into my trip, however, my privates didn't feel quite right. One of our buyers sent me to her doctor, who told me I had gonorrhea and sent me back to my hotel with a prescription for antibiotics. Meanwhile, the kid who infected me would, years later, become chairman of a leading upscale national retail chain. And no, I never kissed and told. That wasn't my style.

Was that single night of pleasure worth the pain that followed? Probably not. But I could no longer ignore the fact that something was missing in my life. I had committed adultery with a man and done so willingly, enthusiastically, with eyes wide open. As a practicing Catholic, I felt obligated to make things work with Terry, who hated living in New York probably more than she loved me. What I didn't understand was how I'd failed her. We had two beautiful children. She drove an expensive Mercedes sedan. We lived in a spacious apartment with a view of Riverside Park, and she had a cleaning lady, beautiful clothes, invitations to galas, and more. But Terry didn't like or want any of it. And the more I worked and provided and lavished, the more she marinated in her unhappiness. She wasn't interested in wealth or glamor or travel; she wanted to go home to Texas.

Despite my best efforts to fix our disintegrating marriage, I had a feeling there was no going back to the way things were before I cheated. A door had swung open for me, and I wasn't sure how to close it.

131

CHAPTER 14

In 1968, a young designer named Ralph Lauren made an appointment to show us his new collection of men's ties. At the time, he worked for Beau Brummel, a necktie manufacturer whose star shone brightly in the 1940s but dimmed by the 1960s, and he was shopping his first solo line, called Polo, to retailers and manufacturers.

That he arrived at the showroom with a large briefcase full of silk ties didn't interest me at all; we made clothes for women, after all. Then he opened it and spread out his designs. They weren't just any old ties, and they were definitely not ties that men wore to work or dinner every day in any city across America. What he had was a collection of big, wide ties in vivid colors. Solids and stripes. Paisley and checks. It was time for a change in American fashion, he said; why not start with men's ties? One look at his innovative collection, and I agreed.

"These are terrific," Mr. Blauner said, picking up one tie, then another. "We'll take all of them."

Even though Suzy Perette was a womenswear company, we had an entire room filled with gifts to offer buyers and retail executives in exchange for their business or, at the very least, their attention. Ralph Lauren's Polo ties were a smart addition to our arsenal; not all buyers, customers, or important people—important to us—were women.

Gift-giving was another aspect of doing business in retail, and I admired Mr. Blauner for his discipline in getting things done. He lived by many mottos, but one I remember was "Get them to take as much as you can." Enticements in exchange for a leg up on the competition was an easy way to handle things. Say a buyer from Sakowitz or Bloomingdale's mentioned admiring a ceramic vase in a certain art gallery or a silver bracelet or even the latest fancy calculator on the market. The next day, she (or he) would get a surprise delivery at the office or at home, courtesy of Suzy Perette.

Whether it was a mink coat, a painting from Galerie Félix Vercel, or a case of champagne, I handled the purchase and distribution. I had Gucci purses stacked up for assistant buyers at department stores, Steuben glass for the buyers at the buying offices, tons of high-end stuff—let's call it payola—and I was in charge of it all.

Not that every buyer welcomed our tactics; many sent our gifts back with a *"Thank you, but I can't accept this"* note. Many, however, accepted them with a combination of gratitude and glee. The buyer from Bonwit Teller, with whom I had a testy relationship, happily took whatever we handed out: a mink coat, a painting, an expensive silk scarf, a handbag. I had no idea why Mr. Blauner showered her with gifts and attention every time she came sniffing around the showroom; the woman was demanding, rude, prone to public outbursts, and ugly as homemade sin. And while Bonwit Teller ranked high on the client list, it wasn't the only game in town. One could argue that because she bought generously from Suzy Perette throughout the year—a sign that she had lots of open-to-buy money at her disposal—she deserved special treatment. But really, how much was any womenswear manufacturer expected to put up with for strategic placement at a luxury retailer? Didn't we have to draw the line somewhere? Apparently not. As I discovered during a trip to Paris, the line was more of a suggestion than a full stop.

My boss cut corners here and there in his business with inexpensive fabric and accessories, but when it came to travel he never went cheap. On this particular trip to the City of Light in May 1970, we planned to visit every boutique of note, buy whatever items were hot, take them home, and copy them. It wasn't a couture trip, as the spring shows happened in early March, but somehow the Bonwit buyer wound up tagging along with us. Her presence was like a dull toothache, constant and irritating; I decided to ignore her and focus instead on the fashion. As always, Mr. Blauner booked us first-class accommodations, this time a suite at the Ritz, where one of my favorite movies, *Love in the Afternoon*, was filmed. I swooned a little when I walked into my room. Not only did it have a view of the Place Vendôme, but there were also French doors opening onto a long outdoor terrace. We had no commitments until dinner, so I decided to unpack, freshen up, and explore the private terrace. After all, it was a sunny, blue-sky day in Paris, and I couldn't resist the siren call of a stroll.

How I wish I had. I stepped out onto the terrace and walked the length of it to get a better look at the Tuileries Gardens in the distance. That's when I made the mistake of glancing in the last window. I can't believe I didn't turn to stone. There was Mr. Blauner, standing in the middle of the room with his pants around his ankles, and the buyer from Bonwit Teller on her knees giving him a blow job. I nearly shrieked. Fortunately, their eyes were closed—mine would have been too if that gargoyle of a woman had her mouth around my penis. I, on the other hand, didn't close mine fast enough. It took me years to exorcise that image from my memory.

My disagreements with the buyer from Bonwit Teller eventually blossomed into all-out war. Every time a competitor like Lord & Taylor or Bloomingdale's ran an ad for a Suzy Perette design in any publication, she called me in a rage, acting as if I'd personally insulted her. Really, she was angry that she hadn't thought of it first. Or maybe that Mr. Blauner hadn't told her about the ad or the new designs. She was a special customer, but not our only customer, and this sent her over the edge sometimes. She also resented my close relationships with people like Kal Ruttenstein at Lord & Taylor, because when push came to shove, she knew I would shove her out the door if I could. What did she expect? A ticker tape parade for yelling at me?

The year before my first brush with infidelity, I came up with a dress inspired by a collection titled Parisiennes that was on display at the Town Shop. Mine was a simple, ingenious design—a front, a back, and two sleeves—and so easy to make that Mr. Blauner thought nobody would buy it. Where had I heard that before?

"Don't worry, they'll buy it," I said. "Because they're going to buy this beautiful printed fabric."

Kal and I wanted to run a full-page ad in the Sunday edition of the *New York Times*, which was going to cost a bundle. Since Lord & Taylor wouldn't pay for the whole thing, we had to cobble together financing from other sources. I went in search of a potential sponsor. DuPont, which had recently come out with a jersey fabric they wanted to promote, offered me as much fabric as I needed and twenty thousand dollars toward the ad; in turn, the ad would publicize DuPont's fabric. It was a you-scratch-my-back-I'll-scratch-yours deal for everyone.

The ad ran with a full-color sketch of my design. In the weeks that followed, we couldn't print the fabric fast enough to keep up with demand and eventually sold more than twenty thousand units of my dress. When she found out about the ad and the dress, the buyer from Bonwit Teller flipped out. She called our office, demanding to talk to me only to hear that I was unavailable, so she railed at the receptionist instead. It was bad enough that Lord & Taylor beat her to the finish line; they were also making money off my dress and with my help. Fortunately, I had the good sense to warn the switchboard she might call and, in a moment of delicious spite, asked them to take a message until further notice.

*

Mr. Blauner was a mass of contradictions. He could be mercurial, irrational, and ruthless. He was allegedly a serial philanderer who probably didn't limit himself to the buyer from Bonwit Teller. But he was also an amazing mentor who taught me how to get things done, when to go cheap and when not to, and gave generously of his time and money.

In 1965, when my son, Kevin, was old enough to start elementary school, Mr. Blauner suggested that we apply to Dalton, an exclusive private school on the Upper East Side. He sang its praises and made a call to ensure that Kevin's application would get a thorough review. We were thrilled when he was offered a spot in the kindergarten class, until the fine print in the contract noted that tuition was five thousand dollars a year. I was making a decent salary, but that price tag was too high for our single-income family. I shared the news with Mr. Blauner and told him we were considering other options like parochial school.

"We are very grateful for all your help," I said. "But it's more than we can afford. Maybe, when we have enough saved up, we'll reapply."

"What does it cost to go to Dalton these days?" he asked, although in hindsight, I think he already knew.

"About five thousand a year," I said. "I'm sure it's a first-class education, but we don't have that kind of money."

He opened the bottom drawer in his desk, pulled out a paper bag, and tossed it to me. Inside was a roll of bills. Hundreds, maybe thousands, of dollars.

"What is this for?" I said. "What am I supposed to do with this?"

"Pay the tuition."

And that was that. He left no room for a gracious refusal. That September, Kevin started kindergarten at Dalton.

A year later, Mr. Blauner surprised me again. Every Thursday evening, we invited a different group of buyers and editors to dinner at La Grenouille. One night, we were leaving when it started to rain. Ever tried to find a cab in New York in the rain? It's a losing proposition. In any case, I had my car and offered to drive Mr. Blauner and a few others home. It was a tight fit in my 1965 white Mustang, but everyone got home dry. The next day, Mr. Blauner called me into his office.

"What color do you want?" he said without preamble.

"What color of what do I want?" I asked. "What are you talking about, Mr. Blauner?"

"What color Mercedes do you want?" he snapped. "I can't have you driving important people around in that toy car of yours. Tell me what color you want, and I'll take care of it."

A week later, I was driving a four-door brown Mercedes sedan. And while I now had plenty of room for school carpools and Suzy Perette customers, I didn't get rid of the Mustang; I kept it in a garage around the corner from our apartment and occasionally took it out for a spin. I drove that little car more often during the summer months, when Terry absconded to Houston with the children. On weekends, if I wasn't working (which I usually was), I took it out to the country, rolled down the windows, and drank in the fresh air.

Sometimes, however, the unbearable weight of loneliness threatens to drag you down. That's when common sense jumps in the back seat to enjoy the ride, and temptation can lead you off the straight and narrow and right into someone else's bed.

My first real affair began during the summer of 1971. An executive from the May Company's New York buying office wanted to discuss an idea she had for a promotion with top sportswear, dress, coat, and eveningwear designers. She invited Mr. Blauner and me to lunch at a Midtown restaurant to discuss how we might help each other. I had just sat down when a tall, lanky beauty walked up to our table.

"Hi, I'm Dawn Mello," she said in a voice that could have melted butter.

She introduced the handsome guy accompanying her as a merchandising manager, and we sat down to order food and talk business. About halfway through lunch, I felt a foot pressing against mine. At first, I thought the merchandising manager was playing footsies with me, which would have been flattering. But it was a long, narrow foot—too long and narrow to belong to a man. Obviously, it wasn't Mr. Blauner, so that left only Dawn Mello, who was sitting across from me. Surprise must have shown on my face, because she gave me a knowing smile, even as she emphasized the importance of personal appearances over Mr. Blauner's protests.

"Look, if you want to do business in America, you have to build a name that people recognize and want to buy from," she said, sliding her foot up my pant leg. "Personal appearances can make all the difference."

I hadn't been looking for trouble, but here it was, ordering veal scaloppini and a green salad.

Dawn and I started out as friends. Foot foreplay aside, I made it clear that nothing was going to happen between us. We were both married, and I wasn't really the cheating type. Over the next month or so, we developed a great working relationship with one successful promotion after another. We spent time together planning events, exchanging ideas, enjoying a comfortable banter. I should have known—Who am I kidding? Of course I knew—when she showed up at my apartment one night with a small package of veal—the reference didn't hit me until later—wrapped in butcher paper that our friendship was about to shift gears. We cooked a simple dinner, then we made love for the first time. Looking back, it seemed inevitable. I was alone and hungry for intimacy; she—well, I didn't know if she was unhappily married or what—wanted me, and that was enough.

That night—and every night we were together—I told her I wouldn't leave my wife. I probably said it as much to reassure myself as anything else. Dawn was smart, sexy, and fabulous, and the longer we carried on, the harder it became to imagine life without her. I didn't mean to, but I fell in love. Once my family returned from Houston, we found ways to sneak around. I would take a detour from LaGuardia Airport on my way home from a business trip and meet her for an afternoon tryst. When Terry and the children were away, she would come to our apartment. In between our romantic moments, we talked fashion and art and appreciated each other's company. Only after things came to an unexpected, abrupt end did I understand how hard I'd fallen for her.

We had been seeing each other for about a year when one day she stopped taking my calls. Just like that. I called her office and spoke to her assistant, but she wouldn't put me through. Dawn was in a meeting; Dawn was in Chicago or at lunch. This went on for weeks, until I finally gave up, miserable and confused. Maybe she got tired of me, or maybe I ignored the signs that our relationship had run its course. It wasn't until the early 1990s, nearly twenty years later, that we reconnected. By then she was president of Bergdorf Goodman and a powerful figure in the fashion world, while I had left Suzy Perette and started my own successful company in Dallas. During one of my trips to New York, Dawn and I got together for lunch. Over coffee and a Viennese pastry, she offered me prime space for a Victor Costa boutique in Bergdorf's, a coup for any independent designer and manufacturer. That boutique, which cost me a bundle to build out, ended up being a cash cow for my company. And while I was grateful to Dawn for her support and our rediscovered friendship, she never did tell me why, without explanation, she left me dangling, with my heart in my hands. Every time I asked, she smiled and changed the subject. Sadly, she passed away in 2020, so I'll never know.

The same year Dawn and I met, St. Thomas High School in Houston decided to put together a fashion show to raise money for the school and some of its programs. And because I was a fashion designer and a graduate of the class of 1953, they wanted to feature my designs. Needless to say, I was honored and elated, and I remember thinking that my mother would want a front-row seat. When the president of the St. Thomas Mother's Club, which was organizing the event, flew up to New York to meet with Mr. Blauner, he responded with "I can't spare him." Meaning me. He couldn't spare me for a show of my designs in my honor!

At first, I was ready to raise holy hell. But then Robert Sakowitz, head of one of the most esteemed retailers in Houston, got involved. He asked Mr. Blauner what it would cost to get me down there to host the show, even for a day or two, and that's when I understood my boss's initial refusal was part of a game. I almost fainted when Mr. Blauner suggested something in the range of one hundred fifty thousand dollars, which would be about one million dollars today. My time was valuable, but was it really worth that much? Even I didn't think so.

Robert didn't blink. He didn't storm out or accuse my boss of being a greedy bastard—at least, not that I know of. Instead, he cut a deal and returned to Houston having ordered many dresses to display and sell in the Sakowitz stores. Thanks to his generosity and intervention, the first Mother's Club fashion show went off without a hitch. It was a sellout crowd at the Westin Oaks Hotel, which also debuted in 1971. That first show was me and my clothes, and a group of mothers and top Houston models wearing them. I emceed the show that year, the following year, and the year after that. Twenty-five years flew by before I finally stepped down as host. And the show? It lives on.

Over the next couple of years, despite occasional turmoil in my personal life, I had little to complain about. Business was booming, I was busier than ever, and my designs for Suzy Perette were selling well in department stores all over the country. By 1973, I had appeared on several daytime television shows like *What's My Line?* and *To Tell the Truth.* I'd been written up in magazines and newspapers, hosted events from coast to coast, and copied some of the finest designers in the history of fashion. All of which is to say that life was, for the most part, very good. Of course, that's when the bottom fell out.

Over breakfast one morning, Terry announced she was taking our daughter and moving back to Houston. Adrienne, then twelve years old, suffered from chronic asthma. The pediatrician told Terry that the mediocre air quality in New York probably made things worse for her fragile lungs, but Houston, where mold and pollen lurked in abundance, seemed to me like an asthma attack waiting to happen. Our son, Kevin, did not want to leave his school or his friends and dug in his heels to make the point. He refused to go.

Terry had never found her footing in New York, either among the private school mothers or my fashion industry friends; she remained an outsider with no apparent interest in making any social headway. Our daughter's health gave her the excuse she needed to pack up and move in with her parents. But Kevin was happy in New York, and I couldn't abandon my job with the snap of her fingers. I asked Terry to wait until summer, when the kids would be out of school and we could talk things through, perhaps negotiate some kind of arrangement that all four of us could live with. She refused, saying she'd waited fourteen years to get the hell out, and she didn't want to wait a minute longer. On a brisk morning in late March 1973, they boarded a Continental Airlines flight from JFK to Houston, leaving our fourteen-year-old son and me alone in the apartment on Riverside Drive.

CHAPTER 15

In the retail business, relationships can make or break a deal. Mr. Blauner understood this and lived by the philosophy that you could never have enough friends. He also made a point of telling me which buyers or retail executives I should get chummy with. As an even-tempered ray of sunshine in an industry full of storm-cloud prima donnas, I could happily socialize and schmooze with almost anyone—the buyer from Bonwit Teller being the exception. It was a rare and valuable skill, and my boss made the most of it.

Before long, I had built a network of contacts and made friends like Kal Ruttenstein and Joan Crawford, both of whom were buyers at Lord & Taylor—Kal at the Town Shop, which sold daytime womenswear, and Joan at the eveningwear boutique on the same floor. She and I met through Kal, became friends—Mr. Blauner always said you can never have too many of those—and remained close for many years.

Joan was funny, smart, and enormously entertaining, with opinions on everything from clothes and people to food and art. As a buyer, she regularly called me to request evening gowns for her department, saying that my designs and reputation—I wasn't Yves Saint Laurent, but I had a large, loyal following—would bring in the shoppers. Honey for the flies, she said. That was Joan, sweet-talking and straight to the point. So when I got a call from the switchboard operator that Joan Crawford was on the line, I assumed she was calling to discuss a new clothing order. The conversation went something like this:

"Hi Joanie, how are you today?" I asked. "What's new?"

"Do I know you?" came an unfamiliar, imperious voice.

"Isn't this Joan Crawford?" I said, not sure whether to be confused or concerned.

"No, this is THE Joan Crawford."

As in that was all the response I needed because I was talking to THE Joan Crawford, acclaimed actress and diva, not some unknown who happened to share her name. I recognized the voice from those long-ago Friday nights at the Majestic Theatre with my mother. This was the Joan Crawford of films, the Joan Crawford for whom I designed and made paper-doll dresses as a little boy. THE one and only Joan Crawford.

"I saw an evening dress in a Bonwit Teller advertisement," she continued. "When I called the store, they told me they were completely sold out and wouldn't be getting any more. They said it was one of your designs, Mr. Costa. You are Victor Costa, aren't you? I want one of those dresses."

It took me a minute to realize she was talking about a dress I copied from a Pucci print, a brilliant, colorful number that was out of stock in a few weeks. Sometimes you hit the right note at the right time.

"Mrs. Crawford, I'm so sorry Bonwit is out of that dress," I said. "Let me see what I can do. How should I get in touch?"

She rattled off her personal phone number and hung up. I went in search of Mr. Blauner, who was in the cutting room, flirting with Giulietta, the fitting model.

"You'll never guess who just called!" I said. "Joan Crawford. The actress, not the buyer."

"Is she still alive?" he said, sounding as if I'd interrupted an important meeting.

"Well, she wants the dress in the new Bonwit ad, so yes."

I called all over town to see if anyone had the dress. Here was my chance to have a screen legend wear one of my dresses, and the damn thing was sold out everywhere. The only solution was to make one. I called her back, told her I would cut a new dress for her myself, and have it ready within the week.

"I'll deliver it in person," I said. "Door-to-door service."

"That's very kind," she said. "Let me know when you're coming by, and you can stay for a drink."

A few days later, I called to let her know the dress was ready. Since it was evening, I decided to bring Kevin with me. He was a darling boy, a real charmer with the older ladies. We arrived at her apartment on the Upper East Side, and she invited us in for a drink. We walked in to find everything encased in plastic. There were no carpets or rugs, and every sofa and chair was covered in clear plastic. I found out later that she was a well-known germaphobe. That said, she was very gracious and welcoming. And when Kevin asked for a Coca-Cola, she managed to keep her temper.

"We only serve Pepsi here," she said.

Well of course they did. Her husband was the chairman and CEO of Pepsi's parent company, PepsiCo. She offered Kevin a glass of water instead, and then invited us to stay for dinner. It was a simple meal, as I recall, soup and sandwiches followed by chocolate cake and ice cream, all served on silver platters by sturdy ladies wearing the gray and white uniforms of domestic help. What a marvelous evening we had with THE Joan Crawford, who entertained us with stories of her life as a Hollywood actress. When we left her apartment around ten o'clock, I assumed our adventure with the A-list diva was a one-off, soon to become a unique conversation starter at dinner parties. I could see it unfolding over cocktails or a salad course.

"Did you hear about my dinner with Joan Crawford? Yes, THE Joan Crawford." And so on.

Then, a few weeks later she called me to ask another favor. She was being honored as one of Hollywood's legendary actresses in a series at The Town Hall in New York. The series also included Bette Davis, Myrna Loy, and Lana Turner, and she wanted me to make a dress for her to wear, one that would outshine her rivals. I designed a long-sleeved, floor-length black sheath in silk taffeta. It was sophisticated, sexy, and spectacular. At the final fitting, I asked her what shoes she planned to wear with the dress.

"Don't worry about it," she said. "I have shoes."

"Mrs. Crawford, I'm not doing the hem on this dress until you show me the shoes you're going to wear," I said. "Depending on how high the heels are, it will affect the hem length."

She asked her assistant to fetch a particular pair of black silk shoes from her closet. The woman returned with what should have been a stunning pair of evening shoes, except that every bit of silk, from heel to toe, was shrink-wrapped in clear plastic.

"You can't wear these shoes, Mrs. Crawford," I said.

"You don't tell me what to wear," she huffed.

"Honestly, you can't wear these shoes," I repeated. "The audience will laugh you off the stage. If you walk out in those shoes, they'll see them and they will laugh."

That got her attention. She condescended to go shopping with me the next day at Bergdorf's, where she bought another pair of expensive black silk shoes. She wore them sans plastic to the event. I don't know if she wore them ever again. More likely than not, they ended up in the trash.

Sometime that fall, I got a piece of news that upended my professional life. In our weekly staff meeting, Mr. Blauner announced that his son's company, Jeunesse, had filed for bankruptcy and shut down, and that Richard would be joining Suzy Perette before the new year. In other words, the son who abandoned the family to form a now-failed competitor was coming home with his tail between his legs. Did my boss really think I could work with a spoiled brat who so easily gave his father the finger? Did Richard expect to be my equal in the company, or my new boss? Did he think he could walk in and start designing clothes? The more I thought about possible scenarios, the more I wanted to bolt screaming for the exit.

Mr. Blauner must have sensed my disappointment because he enlisted his wife to give me a pep talk over dinner at their apartment one night. She told me that I would love working with Richard. He was a new man, no longer the arrogant, overconfident boy who left on a moment's notice. He was humble, hard-working, blah, blah, blah, and so on. Would I stay and guide him, offer my wisdom and years of experience? They were a mother's words about a prodigal son. I couldn't blame her, but I didn't think for a moment the new world order would work for me. Although line for line promotions had been dead for several years, I still copied my favorite designers like Oscar de la Renta, Geoffrey Beene, and Emanuel Ungaro, among others, and those collections sold very well. I also had my own line of original designs. Would that change with Richard in the mix? So many questions and no clear answers. I smiled and told Mr. Blauner I would think about it.

A few days after dinner at the Blauners, I flew to Houston to visit Terry and Adrienne and to attend the St. Thomas fashion show. I'd been there only a day when a man named Donald Stull called me. He owned the Ann Murray Company, a Dallas-based manufacturer that made womenswear and counted some big department stores among its customers. Mr. Stull knew me by reputation; he had seen my collections and admired both my couture copies and original designs. Was there any chance I might be interested in a business partnership that involved leading their design team? The day after the fashion show, I hopped a plane to Dallas to meet with him, spurred by the possibility that this opportunity might offer a way out of Suzy Perette and, in doing so, solve the Richard Blauner problem for me.

If I went by appearances, I would have made a beeline back to the airport. The company was on the third floor of a mostly unoccupied building near the Greyhound bus terminal in downtown Dallas. Fortunately, I had seen Ann Murray's various lines, which were serviceable if far from the fantasy and froth I envisioned for my own designs. I knew I could do better, but it gave me a starting point. That got me thinking about what I wanted to do and where I wanted to be in a few years—and it wasn't working with or for Richard Blauner. My mind made up, I flew home on a Sunday, went into the office on a Monday, and told Mr. Blauner I was leaving the company.

"I have an offer to be lead designer and a partner in a company in Dallas," I said. "And I've accepted it. This is my two weeks' notice."

Of course, I thanked him for taking a chance on me all those years ago and for everything he had done for me and my family. My gratitude fell on furious ears. I should have foreseen his reaction; Mr. Blauner hated surprises, unless they benefited the company or his personal bank account. I guess he thought I would stay at Suzy Perette until I dropped dead or collected Social Security, whichever came first.

"You'll be back in a month," he called to me as I walked out the door—actually, trotted, in case he decided to hurl a pair of scissors at me—for the last time. "And you'll be begging for your job!"

Not exactly the nostalgic parting of the ways I'd hoped for. I knew then that I'd sooner beg for coins on the corner than ask Mr. Blauner for a job. It was a sad end to a glorious, successful period in my life.

On December 17, 1973, I boarded a flight to Dallas with Kevin and two shopping bags full of patterns of every hot seller I made during my years at Suzy Perette. I managed that because whenever we cut a sample, we slipped marking paper between the pieces of fabric. Once it was cut, I had my assistant, Lucrezia, write down the pattern number on the paper and put it in an envelope, which I then took home. It was a clever move. Over the years, I amassed a large collection of patterns and stored them in a closet. Like insurance. You have it because you never know what might happen. And there I was, with two bags of insurance stowed under the seat in front of me.

Halfway through the flight, I remembered it was my birthday. I was thirty-eight years old, and the rest of my family was waiting for us to join them for Christmas in Houston. I had rented a small apartment in Dallas. In the new year, Kevin would start at a new school, and I would start my new job. Terry and Adrienne planned to move to Dallas in June, when I hoped we would begin writing a happier chapter in our relationship.

Mary and Russell Costa

The Costa family, from left to right: Donald, Russell (father), Eva, Mary (mother) and Victor

The Costa children, from left to right: Eva, Donald and Victor

Victor and his sister, Eva

Class picture, Holy Name grammar school

Above: Victor and Terry Costa
on their wedding day in Paris

Right: Terry Costa with son,
Kevin, on his christening day

On this page: Sketches
by Victor Costa

On this page: Sketches by Victor Costa

Adrienne, Victor and Kevin Costa. Photo by Gittings Photography

Jerry Ann and
Victor Costa on their
honeymoon in Paris

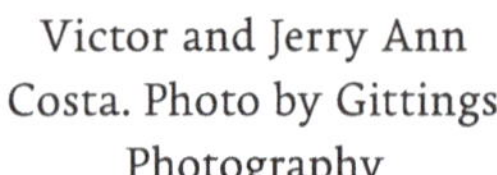

Mary Costa and her son,
Victor Costa

Victor and Jerry Ann
Costa. Photo by Gittings
Photography

On this page: Photos from the Texas Fashion Collection, University of North Texas College of Visual Arts and Design

Left: Photo courtesy of Anna Smith

On this page: Photos courtesy of Anna Smith from the Texas Fashion Collection, University of North Texas College of Visual Arts and Design

On this page: Photos from the Texas Fashion Collection, University of North Texas College of Visual Arts and Design

PART THREE:

Dallas,
1973-1995

CHAPTER 16

Of all the places I saw myself living, Dallas wasn't on the list. Then again, how many of us wind up where we planned to? Once I got over the shock of uprooting our lives, I realized we hadn't landed in a one-horse backwater. Not by any stretch. Dallas had money, a vibrant social scene and cultural life, and a fabulous collection of museums and wealthy art patrons to support them. Honestly, it was a terrific city to move to, but it wasn't New York, which didn't matter as much to me as it did to Kevin.

Our son was desperately unhappy to be yanked away from his friends, his school, and the only place he'd ever called home only to be plopped down in a new city and a new life in the middle of his freshman year. Who could blame him for being sad and furious? I encouraged him to try out for sports teams and join clubs. I told him things would get better once he started meeting people. I reminded him that he was at one of the best schools in Dallas, and that would make a difference. What a crock. I forgot there are bullies and monsters every-where, even—or maybe especially—in the storied cloisters of high-priced private schools.

A couple of months into the new semester, Terry and I got a call from the headmaster summoning us to his office. It turned out that some of Kevin's classmates had been giving him a hard time. One thing led to another, which led to our son's nose being broken in a scuffle.

"Nothing like this ever happened to Kevin at Dalton," I

snapped at the suited head of school.

He nodded and apologized several times, declaring that the boys responsible would be punished. "And I think we can all agree on the importance of keeping this incident private, can't we?" he said. "It would be a shame for a few bad apples to tarnish our school's reputation."

I couldn't believe what I was hearing. Our son's nose had been broken by some of his classmates, and this twerp was worried about negative publicity. Terry and I left then to find Kevin and get him to a doctor. As we were walking out, I told the headmaster I'd let him know whether or not we were taking this issue to the newspapers. I like to imagine he didn't sleep much that night.

In the end, we did not make a stink or go to the newspapers, thinking that might turn a bad situation into something worse for Kevin. Instead, we looked around for a month or so and found a different school, where he was much happier. But those first few months in Dallas interrupted his world, and I don't think he ever forgave me for it.

My mother taught me to make the best of what we're given. That, and don't whine because people can't stand whiners. I agree; life is too short to make room for whiners. In any case, I walked into Ann Murray ready to work hard and make the best of it. Fortunately, I had the patterns I'd brought with me, so I started producing clothes as soon as I could. I wanted to have a collection ready for the spring shows in New York. Two months wasn't much time—people must have thought I was delirious—but I would make it happen. I had to.

Two weeks into it, I went to see Mr. Stull, founder of the company, and said we needed to rethink things. Knocking myself out for a company that produced what was, in my opinion, mediocre womenswear didn't seem like a smart use of my energy or creative abilities. My designs were better and brought a certain sophistication that was otherwise lacking in Ann Murray's clothing lines. I know how it sounds, but sometimes the truth is just that. Without insulting the quality of his product, I suggested that we tweak our professional arrangement by launching a line under my name. I explained that a separate line would be complementary, not competitive, because I would offer dresses at first and possibly expand into eveningwear if things went well. I must have sounded very convincing, because Mr. Stull approved my plan without much back and forth, in time for me to pull something together for the spring shows.

While the new Victor Costa line was being cut and sewn, I called the York Hotel on Seventh Avenue and booked a suite to use as a showroom. I planned to stay in our apartment, which we hadn't yet vacated. That we were still paying rent on a place we no longer lived in was another example of my occasional inability to face reality. My practical self knew deep down we weren't moving back to New York. Not anytime soon, anyway. But another part of me secretly hoped the move to Dallas was nothing more than an intermission between acts, and we would return to the main stage of New York once all the guests were back in their seats, so to speak.

In the spring of 1974, I flew up to New York for Fashion Week with a collection of twenty-five dresses and Mr. Stull's son-in-law, an executive at the company. With the help of Kal Ruttenstein, who had moved uptown to Saks Fifth Avenue, I organized a show in our suite at the York Hotel. I didn't know what to expect, maybe good reviews and enough sales to justify keeping my own line. Instead, I won the lottery. Fashion writers praised the beauty and affordability of my designs; buyers raved over this dress or that one, then placed orders for thousands of pieces. We sold out of everything in a week.

One dress was such a crowd-pleaser that, by the time we were back in Dallas and in production, we couldn't make it fast enough even though our production facility was local.

That was one of three dresses I cut from another inexpensive DuPont jersey fabric. They were straightforward designs with two sleeves, two front pieces, two back pieces, and a zipper, but the star of the trio had Swarovski crystal buttons down the front. That little bit of bling transformed a simple dress into a frock that sparkled like a movie star on the red carpet; the forty-five-dollar price tag made it the bargain of the season. No wonder we had to hustle to keep up with demand. When the dust (and the dresses) finally cleared out, I calculated that we did about one million dollars in sales from my first post-Suzy Perette collection. Nearly fifty years later, the thought of it still makes me smile.

Ann Murray had two showrooms in the Apparel Mart. While it doesn't exist anymore, the Apparel Mart was, at the time, the nerve center of the Dallas wholesale fashion trade and one of a handful of apparel centers around the country. Buyers came from as far away as Asia and Europe to browse the seasonal collections. Not long after my triumph at the spring shows in New York, Mr. Stull converted one of the company's Apparel Mart spaces into a Victor Costa showroom.

With a room of my own, I began holding shows every weekday at two o'clock. If you wanted a seat, you had to make a reservation; otherwise, you might find yourself standing in the back. I emceed every show, chatting with the audience and introducing each piece and the model who wore it, and I often sang a favorite tune to kick things off. I wanted my collections—whether original or inspired by other designers—to be taken seriously, but I saw no harm in keeping the mood festive and fun. It paid off. In a few short months, my shows became must-attend favorites on the Dallas fashion industry calendar.

By 1975, about a year and a half after our move to Dallas, my business within Ann Murray was doing so well that I had enough money to start my own company. I made Mr. Stull an offer, which he accepted, and folded Ann Murray's assets—

minus the clothing lines—into my new business, Victor Costa, Inc. It was a thrilling moment for me, the boy who aspired to design clothes that made women look and feel beautiful. I savored my accomplishment for a day or two before jumping back into the frenzy of responsibilities that came with owning and running a business. I hired an assistant and an accountant and kept most of the employees who worked in production. Beyond that, I focused on what I did best: design and sales and promoting the hell out of my collections.

My efforts paid off. Before long, I was traveling around the country to introduce my clothing lines and host shows at various department stores and high-end retailers. During a visit to I. Magnin in San Francisco, where I was emceeing a fashion show for an audience of hundreds, a staffer pulled me aside to say I had an emergency phone call. I excused myself and went running, afraid something had happened at home. It was my accountant—actually the accountant I'd inherited when I took over Ann Murray—demanding that I get back to Dallas and run my business. Of the strange experiences I've had in my life, an employee ordering me to come home ranked up there.

"I am not coming right now," I said. "This customer bought hundreds of our dresses and, as part of our agreement, I'm doing a series of appearances and shows in the store. We can discuss things when I get back."

I wrapped up my visit, still mystified by the phone call, and went home. His intention became clear to me when he came into my office the day after I returned. He told me that I didn't know what I was doing and that I needed to stay put and run the company.

"I design the clothes and make the patterns," I said, incensed. "Our production guy makes the clothes. Why do I have to be here?"

"You can't do all that alone. You need somebody to help you," he said. "I want you to hire my son."

There it was. All the fuss and drama to make it seem like I couldn't run my company because his son wanted a job. I should have fired the accountant on the spot. But I was a soft-hearted pushover, so I agreed to hire his son to visit our production contractors. I took time to train him, showed him how to dress a mannequin and how to compare one of our original pieces to what the contractor was producing to make sure they looked the same. It was an important job that required being out of the office frequently, and this young man fit all the requirements; he was energetic, eager, and unemployed.

Of course, there's a "but" in this story. There was something about my new employee that didn't sit right. Call it intuition or a serendipitous hunch. Whatever it was, I hired a private investigator to find out if I was being perceptive or paranoid.

"I think this kid is taking me for a ride," I told him during our first meeting. "He's been here for several months. He picks up our samples in the morning and comes back at six o'clock claiming that he's visited all these contractors. I don't think it's possible."

The investigator followed the suspect around for a few days before reporting back to me that he was shacking up in a motel every other day with different women when he should have been working. It's not for me to point fingers over someone else's indiscretions; however, he was cheating on company time and paying with the company's dime. Never mind that his wife was pregnant with their first child. What a thankless ass. I sent him packing the day after I found out what he was up to. His father, however, refused to acknowledge the evidence of his son's womanizing during work hours and resigned a week later. That turned out to be a blessing masquerading as an awkward situation.

Not long after our accountant and his son left, I discovered they had been working out how to persuade me to offer the son a twenty-five-percent stake in my company. I remember shaking my head in disgust at the thought, not only because there is little people won't do to get what they want but also because there was a good chance I would have fallen for it. While I'm not an imbecile, some would say I can be a trusting fool. I prefer to think of it as giving people the benefit of the doubt. That time, I managed to emerge with my company and my pride in one piece.

In the early days of Victor Costa, Inc., the company was housed in a small building that used to be a center for woodworking, with remnants of sawdust lurking in the corners. We cleaned it up, turned it into a dress factory, and did all the designing, cutting, and modeling. For a while, it was all we needed. We were busy, growing, and profitable because we stuck to our formula of couture-style womenswear at affordable prices. When I wasn't working (which was almost never), I found my footing in Dallas society through an orchestra of networks and charitable causes.

One of the most inspired volunteer projects I undertook during that time was an homage to legendary designer Norman Norell. Even those who haven't heard of him would recognize his work. He became famous in the 1940s and 50s for designing no-neckline dresses—considered avant-garde in the day—and sequined mermaid gowns, among other things. With icons like Marilyn Monroe, Judy Garland, and Jacqueline Kennedy among his clients, Norell was sought after by wealthy women in search of glamorous eveningwear. I liked his artful creations so much that whenever I wrote out a guest list to a fantasy dinner party of fashion designers, he got top billing. I came up with the idea to honor him and his work as head of a group of fashion aficionados and collectors affiliated with the Dallas Historical Society.

Actually, it started with the Apparel Mart. A less expensive place for buyers to browse, shop, and schmooze than New

York, it drew big numbers of buyers, not only to shop the seasonal collections but to all manner of shows, nearly one every month. But Dallas wasn't New York or Paris. No place was. That didn't matter to me or many others in the fashion industry; we did very good business there and supported it with the passion of football fans. So when I heard the Dallas Historical Society had a basement full of Norell originals, it got me thinking about the possibilities. Why not assemble a different kind of show to add a little sparkle and wow, and give Apparel Mart visitors a magical fashion experience?

When an article in one of the newspapers mentioned that I was planning a Norell show under the auspices of the Dallas Historical Society, the head of that organization called—and she wasn't happy. She went on and on in an imperious tone about how I didn't have permission to use their name or the gowns in the basement, until I reminded her of the check I'd written to the Society the year before. One hundred thousand dollars, which was a lot in the early 1980s, all of it raised from special events at the Apparel Mart. Did she want the money or not?

"Well," she sputtered. "What's your goal with this show?"

"My goal is to clean you all up," I said. "You have a basement full of dresses you think should be in a collection because they have a designer's name on them. Not all of them will make the cut. You have to purge your collection and get it viable to be museum-worthy."

At the time, the Dallas Historical Society aspired to see its couture collection on display at the Dallas Museum of Art. I offered to use the Norell show as a springboard for just such an exhibit. In my spare time, I solicited Norells from famous women who wore them—Cyd Charisse, Greer Garson, and Dinah Shore, among others—and I rescued more than a dozen dresses from the Historical Society's basement. Once I'd organized the concept and the clothes, I met with the Dallas Museum board and explained how this exhibit could serve as a joint fundraiser for the Museum and the Historical Society. After all, what arts organization turns down the gift of money?

The head of the museum couldn't have been less interested. The administration and board considered apparel to be, in his words, "a desecration of textiles." I wondered what Christian Dior, Coco Chanel, or Charles James would have to say about their designs being labeled "desecrations." Nothing good, I'm sure. After offering a few choice words of my own, which should have included "asshole" but did not, I went to real estate developer and art lover Trammell Crow for help in locating a new venue. He found a facility in downtown Dallas, a round structure with a park-like atmosphere—perfect, I thought, for a parade of mostly mermaid gowns glittering with hand-sewn payettes.

The show received more advance publicity than I could have hoped for, which proved to be a double-edged dagger. I was in New York a week or so before it was due to open when I got a call from the Dallas police informing me that the ground-floor windows at Victor Costa, Inc., had been shattered and a stack of Norell dresses stolen. Luckily, I had already pulled out the dresses we were going to display and taken them to the exhibit space. What remained in our showroom were largely duplicates. The thieves must have thought the dresses were worth something; I wonder how much they made for their trouble.

Years later, a friend called to tell me that Norman Norell's desk was for sale, and did I want to buy it? Absolutely. I bought the desk and eventually turned it into a dining room table. Every time I ate a meal on it, I thought of the great designer. It seemed like a fitting tribute to a man whose work I adored.

The indulgence of projects like the Norell exhibit didn't come along that often. As head of my own company, I spent most of my time working or traveling for work and, by about 1985, the company had grown so much that I did two things:

I hired accounting firm Deloitte, Haskins & Sells to monitor my business, and I met with a young man named John who had been persistently calling me about a job. Given what I'd been through with my first accountant and his son, I was a little wary. But this guy was smart, charming, and, most importantly, an accountant—by his own estimation and his references, a very good accountant. Ledgers, statements, and balance sheets didn't interest me; I was a designer, promoter, and lover of fashion, not a number-cruncher, and I needed someone to handle the finances. So in 1985, I hired John as my first chief financial officer, confident that having both a CFO and a major accounting firm conducting regular certified public audits of the company meant that I was protected, that nothing could go really wrong.

Then, like Alice in Wonderland, the company outgrew the building. Business moved through the seasons at a breathless pace; from one month to the next, orders doubled, then tripled. My employees grumbled about not having enough room to work. On the surface, these were good problems to have, but I could see backlogged orders and irate customers in my future if we didn't do something. With my crazy schedule, when was I going to find new digs?

I didn't have to. John came into work one day saying he'd found a bigger building that met our needs, a former car dealership and showroom with enormous windows everywhere. If I liked it, he said he would make everything—the lease negotiation and the relocation—happen with as little disruption as possible to my routine. It was like having a magician on staff. I toured the seventy-thousand-square-foot building and fell a little in love. John was right; it was perfect. I signed on the dotted line, and we moved in before the next season's collection hit the stores. My own office was spare yet tasteful, with lots of clean lines and white décor, including a white desk on a white-carpeted platform and a row of floor-to-ceiling windows with white plantation shutters. I found it soothing and often used it as a haven from my increasingly turbulent home life.

Work trumped nearly everything. It got me up in the morning and kept me going, lit a fire in my belly when I felt a case of the "poor me's" coming on. I've never had much time or patience for self-pity; nobody wants to hear how bad you've got it because there is always someone who has it worse. So I worked and worked and worked. I produced some dazzling collections—big bows, lots of sparkle, rich colors—that included Victor Costa originals and designs inspired by couture of the moment—that is, copies.

There was never a time when I wasn't copying. Longevity is the most important thing in a fashion career, and you can't be a great fashion designer unless you evolve with the times. So I continued to copy, even though line for line had faded into obscurity nearly twenty years earlier. Some designers didn't appreciate that I copied their designs and sold them for a song compared to couture prices. But how could I resist? They made such magnificent clothes. It seemed a shame that so many women could admire them but not afford them.

I went to Paris, as I always had, for ideas and inspiration, except now I was often persona non grata. Some designers—Ungaro, Oscar, and Lacroix come to mind—positioned security guards at their shows with specific orders to turn me away at the entrance. That's when I got creative, showing up with a roll of hundred-dollar bills in my wallet. Depending on whose show it was, I paid the security guards to look the other way while I went in. A few bills, a nod, and it was "Victor who?"

I usually went in by myself, briefcase in hand, memorized everything I wanted to copy, and then walked out with a group of fashion editors and writers, often from *Vogue* or *Harper's Bazaar*. I remember one editor asking me if I was going to make dresses with the same style of puffy sleeve we had seen at the Ungaro show.

"Of course I am," I said. "I'm going to make whatever is popular and being publicized."

On another occasion, Katie Couric, then co-host of the *Today* show, interviewed me during the spring shows in Paris. We met on the Pont Neuf at nine o'clock in the morning to talk about fashion and my success in making couture knock-offs that made women feel like a million dollars at a reasonable price. How many designers got to talk on national television about the same designers who would love to kick me out of their shows, ass first? What a great, fun time that was!

At home, the picture was less than perfect. From the outside looking in, we seemed like a family who had it all: a house in University Park, two children at private school, and a wife who had the luxury of not working. The reality was that our daughter was the youngest boarder at a school in San Antonio; our son resented us for moving him to Texas; and my relationship with Terry, while not yet on life support, was dying.

As a Catholic, I was taught that if your marriage hit the rocks, you either fixed it or went down with the ship. Given my upbringing and naturally positive outlook on life, I endeavored all along to make things work with Terry. One of my last-ditch efforts before everything fell apart for good was to give her a job. After one of our big orders was canceled and we found ourselves with a load of extra dresses, I came up with the idea of opening an outlet store. On those occasions when we had cancelations or overstock, wouldn't it make sense to have a place to sell the merchandise?

When Terry expressed an interest in that end of the business, I hired her to run the store. We set it up in a space on the first floor of our building, three blocks from Neiman Marcus, and started going to work together every day. She seemed to enjoy being in charge and having something to do; for a while, it got her out of bed in the morning and gave her a purpose beyond marriage and motherhood.

But that fleeting sense of satisfaction didn't last. She began finding fault with the clothes I sent down to the store. She didn't like the color of one dress; she wanted to change the buttons on another dress; I should have done this, not that. The constant drizzle of displeasure was just another symptom of the discontent that plagued our marriage, and it wore me down. I stayed because I thought I should; then, one day, I couldn't stand the haranguing and unhappiness anymore.

After twenty-six years of marriage, I gave up and told Terry I was moving out. I came home from work one day, packed a couple of suitcases, and drove away. Not that it was easy. Seeing my wife in tears in the foyer, begging me to give us another chance, nearly undid me. In that second of hesitation, I recalled the bickering and insults that dominated our interactions, tension between us so thick you could choke on it, nights of sleeping in the guest room. We both deserved and wanted happiness in our lives, but not with each other. So I left to find some before it was too late.

CHAPTER 17

My solo summers in New York may have been lonely ones, but now, freed from the struggle of trying to fix my marriage, I found that I loved living alone. I rented a charming apartment with a shoebox-sized terrace overlooking Turtle Creek and furnished it simply, tastefully. I went to work every day happy and came home every night with a smile on my face. It was a slice of heaven I'd dreamed about and, finally, I had it.

I still had Terry, too. She ran the Victor Costa outlet store, and we shared two children, by then young adults, but forever ours. Even so, keeping our interactions civil and scant wasn't easy. Some days, she trumpeted her dissatisfaction to everyone in the store; other days, she called me at the office or the apartment, begging me to move back home. It was emotional whiplash, but I understood—no doubt she did, too—that until we agreed to something legal like divorce, the bad days would forever outnumber the good ones. Strange that despite being so unhappy with each other, neither one of us was ready to officially undo twenty-six years of marriage. Instead, we settled into an uneasy peace with separate addresses.

The truth was that I didn't have much time to think about anything but work. My company was growing at a rate that surprised me. I traveled at least once a week, to New York for shows or to meet with buyers, for personal appearances at stores in Omaha, Phoenix, San Francisco, or Chicago, and to Paris several times a year to find inspiration for my own designs.

The importance of making nice with buyers and shoppers in a small Midwestern city or a bustling East Coast hub, of convincing ladies that my dresses could turn any one of them into a beauty queen, could not be overstated. My life was my work, as it so often had been—and probably always would be. Those women across the country who wanted to feel gorgeous and glamorous, if only for a night, were the cornerstone of my success. Sure, there were the Ivana Trumps and Joan Crawfords, famous names who bought one or a dozen of my designs, wore them once, and then donated them or passed them on to their housekeeper. But it was the ladies from Portland and Pittsburgh and Peoria who loved what I did, and I owed it to them to keep going.

For a while, I had everything I wanted. Travel, work, galas, and gatherings. An apartment of my own. What else could I possibly make room for in my jam-packed life? What was missing that I didn't already have? When I slowed down long enough to think about it, I realized the one thing I didn't have was companionship. Even when Terry and I were still living together unhappily, we made love. It may have been perfunctory, but it was physical contact, closeness of some kind.

Throughout my adult life, I have insisted that marriage is an obligation. People have all kinds of interpretations of what it means to be married, but I believed that when I married Terry and we had children, it was my responsibility to give them as much as I could. Now that I was on my own, I thought back to my night with the Lord & Taylor window dresser and wondered whether the issue of bisexuality was something I should revisit. Funny how things come full circle. When my first girlfriend (yes, eons ago) and I finally consummated our relationship years after we dated, she asked me if I was bisexual. My response? "I don't know. Maybe I'm trisexual. Try anything!"

Not to make light of homosexuality or bisexuality or any sexuality, but I grew up in the 1950s. That was a different century; experimentation wasn't the norm. People were expected to behave a certain way and anyone who didn't was labeled strange or different or deviant. By the 1980s, nearly everything was different. Men weren't walking around in public holding hands yet, but it was a wild, open time compared to the world I'd been raised in. I knew I wasn't gay; I loved and was attracted to women. But I was also attracted to men—or certain men—and for a while, I ignored the desire to explore that side of myself. It may have been a more open society than the one I grew up in, but homosexual relationships, while common in my business, were often kept secret in "polite society." When I finally admitted to myself that I had feelings I wanted to understand and perhaps make peace with, I knew who to call.

I had a friend who was a buyer at Sakowitz in Houston. After dozens of phone calls and more than a few business lunches, dinners, and face-to-face meetings, we became friends. From him, I learned that Houston had a vibrant society of homosexuals, and that some men dressed up like women and threw outrageous, fabulous balls. My inexperience and utter ignorance of that world must have surprised him. Or maybe not. I also found out that he lived with a man, a young man who, after several months or a year, bored him to exasperation. He, in turn, heard about my new living arrangement, my marriage woes, and what to expect in the next season's collection. More puffy sleeves? Sexy statement bows? Brilliant colors and shorter hemlines? A variety of dresses with debutante appeal? I enjoyed his company; he had a way about him that made me feel open and comfortable. It was during one of these tête-à-têtes that I confessed I wanted to explore my sexuality. Did he have any advice?

"As a matter of fact, I know someone who might be able to help you with that," he said. "We will be in Dallas next week. How about dinner?"

We made a date for the following Thursday. When I arrived

at the restaurant, he and a handsome young man, presumably the "someone" he wanted me to meet, were already seated. Turned out it was his live-in boyfriend. When the young man went in search of the restroom, my friend mused aloud that Dallas might suit his soon-to-be-ex. Was my company hiring? If so, maybe John or William or Teddy or Steve—I can't remember his name—could help me figure things out. I didn't know whether to be surprised or grateful.

"You'd be doing me a huge favor." He leaned back in his chair and smiled, looking eerily like the cat that ate the neighbor's canary.

My friend was essentially foisting his lover off on me because why not? He was finished with him, and I hadn't yet begun. It wasn't long before the ex-boyfriend had a job at Victor Costa, Inc., and I had a willing guide to walk me through this strange, seductive new world.

After a few months, I understood why my friend had been so willing to send the boy packing. He was sweet; he radiated the vigor and beauty of youth. Beyond that, though, he didn't have much to offer. He wasn't very bright or articulate, and his greatest preoccupation seemed to be his own good looks. In the end, I let him go—with a glowing reference, of course.

My number-one assistant at the manufacturing facility in Dallas was Carlo. We met at Pratt and remained friends even after I transferred to the University of Houston. Carlo had dreams of being a designer, but he couldn't get a break or find the right opportunity. Or maybe he didn't have the talent. When I heard he had moved to Dallas and was looking for a job, I took him to lunch. Before the ink was dry on the credit card receipt, I'd offered him a position as my design assistant. Aside from Carlo, there was a woman named Regina who kept records of what was coming in and out in terms of piece goods, cost sheets, and things like that, and I always had a few interns who helped out with odd jobs in exchange for learning as much as I could teach them about the fashion business.

This was 1985. I was selling to national and regional retailers. I was in the thick of things at the Dallas Apparel Mart. I was always going, meeting, organizing, and orchestrating; it's not too much of a stretch to stay that I stopped only to eat and sleep. So when the Horchow Collection, a Dallas-based high-end mail-order catalog, approached me about designing a few pieces of women's clothing, I wanted to say no. But my contact at Horchow was a charming woman who loved me and my designs—I remember designing a line of very pretty dresses with matching kerchiefs for them—and also happened to be a dear friend. Close enough that when she asked me for a favor, I didn't have the heart to refuse her.

"There's a young man who says he wants to be a designer," she said during one of our phone calls. "I know his mother, otherwise I wouldn't be asking. Do you think you could take him on as a volunteer or an intern? Maybe teach him a few things about your business?"

It was a big ask, but the idea of introducing a young person to my world inspired the mentor in me. Surely I could squeeze one more activity into my schedule. The following week, a twenty-two-year-old named Clay Cope arrived at my office with enthusiasm to spare and no college degree, eager to launch what he was sure would be his future career. I toured him around the building and left him in the talented hands of Carlo and a few other employees. Over the next couple of months, they trained Clay in the art and mechanics of womenswear design and manufacturing. He learned how to cut a garment, put it together, drape it on a mannequin or a fitting model, and much more.

At first, I checked in on him every now and then; after a while, I dropped by more often to catch up on his progress and secretly admire the scenery. He was a very handsome young man—very young and very handsome. I was nearly thirty years older, but I couldn't deny my interest or my attraction. On one level, the whole thing struck me as preposterous, even laughable. I knew better, didn't I? Here I was, at fifty, mooning over someone who was little more than a boy. And yet, the more time I spent with him, the more I enjoyed his company. Things rolled along like this—me finding excuses to check on Clay's progress—for another month or so. It wasn't ideal, but I got to see him every day. Was it crazy of me to be a little besotted with someone the same age as my daughter? Probably. But the heart has a mind of its own, and mine, ignoring all common sense, set its sights on this guileless, gorgeous young man.

I'm not sure if or how I expected this small, budding thing between us to bloom. I knew what I wanted and hoped he felt the same way, but we didn't get a chance to find out. Not then, anyway. His mother called me one day with an ultimatum: pay her son for the work he did or kiss him goodbye. It was a short, polite conversation. I acknowledged that an independent, adult life required a paid job, not an internship; however, I didn't have the budget to hire another person, especially someone with skimpy work experience. Clay quit the next day. A few weeks later, I heard he'd rebounded nicely with a job as a salesperson at Neiman Marcus. I bet that whatever merchandise he was in charge of selling—men's ties or socks or polo shirts—he sold the hell out of it.

We stayed in touch after he left, which was mostly my doing. I knew where he lived and that he took the bus to work every day. On sunny days, I would drive my Mercedes convertible, top down, past his bus stop and often pull over to offer him a ride. "No problem at all," I would say. Neiman's was on the way to my office. Wouldn't it be nice to catch up? I came up with all kinds of excuses, but he always turned me down, even when it was raining. Then one day, he opened the door and got in.

That's how things began. Slowly at first, then a night here

and there, like two people having an affair. But the more time we spent together, the more we felt like a relationship and not a casual fling. I told myself that he was too young, just as I had when he worked for me. Too young. Too easily taken advantage of by a successful, older man like me. Too inappropriate for someone of my standing and reputation. None of that made any difference. We cared for each other and together decided to see where our feelings would lead us. Clay moved in with me a few months later, with his mother's blessing. At that time, I lived in a townhouse across from the Mansion on Turtle Creek. I had wanted to buy the apartment I moved into when Terry and I first separated, but that didn't work out. In a stroke of odd luck, the townhouse was a better fit for two people.

We carried on like that, with an abundance of discretion and few public appearances. Terry and I were separated, not divorced; it would have been tacky, if not cruel, to flaunt my new, unconventional—and, in some corners, socially unacceptable—relationship around town. I also didn't want to give her an excuse to do anything irrational that might negatively affect me, our children, or Clay. All my efforts were for nothing. When Terry filed for divorce in 1986, she named Clay the co-respondent, or the person with whom I was having an affair. She wanted to get him on the stand and use my adultery as her excuse for divorcing me. Then she contacted a number of gay men I'd met through my work in fashion, saying that she would call them as witnesses to prove I was screwing around. It didn't matter that I hadn't spoken to some of them in years or that I'd never had sex with any of them. I blamed myself. When I moved out, I hadn't requested a legal separation. So she could make as much fuss and trouble as she wanted.

The circus didn't end there. Clay and I were home one evening when there was a loud banging on the front door. That's never a good sign. I approached with caution and peered through the peephole. A dark-haired man, average-looking and of average height, stood on the other side. Without opening the door, I asked who he was and how I could help him. He told me he was a process server, and he had a subpoena for someone named Clay Cope. I didn't utter another word. Clay and I stood there, silent as snow, while the man continued to knock and knock. I wasn't about to open the door and let this stranger hand my partner a subpoena. Terry's handprints were all over this, and it infuriated me. An hour later, the guy gave up and left. Meanwhile, I came up with a plan to get Clay out of town.

That night, I called the same friend who had shared his discarded lover with me the year before and now managed a department store in Scottsdale, Arizona. I explained what was happening and asked for his help. I wanted to get Clay out of town for a while; would he mind having a houseguest? It was unspoken between us, but we both knew he owed me one. He didn't hesitate. Of course Clay could stay with him. When did he plan to come? "Tomorrow," I said. I called and booked a flight to Phoenix, then called the man who did my gardening and offered to pay him to take Clay to the airport the following morning at seven o'clock. Clay's flight didn't leave until lunchtime, but I wasn't taking any chances with the persistent process server.

The gardener arrived a few minutes early, parking his truck around back where anyone waiting in front of the house wouldn't be able to spot him. I briefly explained that a strange man had been bothering Clay, and he was going to visit friends while I dealt with the situation. We got Clay and his suitcase under a tarp in the bed of the truck—as a precaution, I said—and I watched them drive away.

Did I overreact? Probably. But I didn't want Clay to be cross-examined or dragged through the muck by a woman who was, perhaps justifiably, hell-bent on carving out a pound or more of my flesh.

Terry and I were officially divorced later that year. And while she didn't get the satisfaction of parading Clay before a judge, she did get nearly everything she wanted. In truth, it was only fair. I was the one who left, the one who moved out, the one who started a new life without her. In the end, I agreed to give her alimony, child support, and ownership of my outlet store, knowing that once the papers were signed we would both be free to find the happiness we were looking for.

CHAPTER 18

Personal dramas notwithstanding, those were remarkable years. Victor Costa, Inc., was booming, adding new orders and new customers at a pace I could barely keep up with. Department stores like Saks Fifth Avenue, Neiman Marcus, Nordstrom, and I. Magnin carried my lines, as did numerous regional department stores and small boutiques around the country. I made appearances on different local and national television shows to talk about the latest fashions and introduce some of my designs. I was even invited to be a guest on the *Oprah Winfrey Show* in 1989, when my pouf dresses—Christian Lacroix knock-offs that were a big hit with pretty young things—were at the peak of their popularity and getting lots of attention. That was the same year I founded Victor Costa Bridal because, after all, I had mastered the art of designing wedding dresses.

My date to be on *Oprah* started with a call from her booking agent asking me to be a guest on the show. Oprah wanted to interview me because my designs were proving to the fashion world that women's clothing didn't have to be overpriced to be attractive. Could I be there on a certain date at seven o'clock in the morning? Was there any chance I would say no to Oprah? You bet your ass there wasn't. I hopped on a plane the day before my scheduled appearance, arrived in Chicago that night, and was there the next morning, caffeinated and on time. The clothes I'd sent ahead had arrived. After a couple of hours, I asked one of Oprah's people what time I would meet the talk-show queen.

"Oh, Oprah doesn't come in until eleven o'clock, and we're taping a few shows today," he said. "You won't see her until four o'clock."

"Why am I here at seven in the morning?"

"Everyone has to come in ahead of time and get checked in," she said, waving her clipboard.

A few minutes past four o'clock, the great lady came in, took her seat, and motioned for me to join her. When the cameras started rolling, she introduced me to the viewers, then turned back to me. I was all gracious smiles.

"You know, Victor, Ivana is right about you," she said. "The way your clothes look on women is really fantastic, and they're so affordable. You're a gift to America!"

I was so flattered, I probably blushed from my scalp to my toes. That Ivana had given my designs such a glowing review was great publicity back then. As several models emerged from behind the curtain wearing some of my newest designs, Oprah and I chatted about current and future clothing trends, how I became interested in fashion, and what inspired me. At some point, we cut to a commercial, and Oprah leaned over to me.

"Boy, am I in trouble," she said, her professional veneer slipping a little. "The NAACP is giving me an award in Los Angeles on Saturday night, and I don't have anything to wear."

She went on to tell me that her boyfriend had given her a spectacular emerald and diamond necklace and earrings, and she wanted to find an outfit that would show them off.

"What am I going to do?" she said, as if I had an answer wrapped up and ready to go.

Before I could say anything, we were back on the air, and she was all business. Once the interview ended, she thanked me for coming and was on to the next guest before her assistant escorted me downstairs to a car waiting to take me to the airport.

"So Miss Winfrey is going to California?" I asked.

"Yes, the awards ceremony is Saturday night," she said.

In that moment, I knew exactly what I was going to do. I got the name of the hotel where Oprah was staying in Los Angeles and contacted her assistant to get the lady's measurements. Then I called my assistant, Carlo, from the airport and began issuing instructions. We had less than four days to get things done.

"You know the green velvet and satin dress with the matching opera coat?" I said. "Cut the pattern immediately, keep everyone there overnight, and get it finished by tomorrow."

When I arrived back in Dallas later that evening, I went straight to the showroom to see how things were progressing—and I stayed until the work was done some time the following afternoon. The people who worked for me produced a spectacular outfit; I couldn't have been prouder of how we all pulled it off with no warning and little time. Dead tired, I packed the dress and coat as carefully as I would a Lalique vase and overnighted it the following morning to Oprah's hotel in Los Angeles. I wanted it to be waiting for her when she arrived on Friday.

Nobody told me I had to be a logistics whiz to be a fashion designer. I called Carlo on a Monday night and shipped the finished dress and coat on Wednesday morning. I didn't know if Oprah would wear it. She probably had a hundred designers begging her to wear their clothes, and you don't throw on any old frock for a nationally televised event. To me, it was the gesture—the act of letting her know that I remembered what she said—that mattered. That, and the outside chance she might wear my design.

The day before the awards ceremony, I had my feet up—still depleted from the frenzied pace we'd kept up to make the dress—and was going through the mail in my study when the phone rang. In those days, Clay and I lived in a lovely house in Highland Park, and we had a housekeeper who answered the phone, took deliveries, and things like that. Clay must have been out because the housekeeper knocked on the door to my study and said, "You have a phone call, Mr. Costa."

"Please tell them I'm resting, and I'll call back," I said. "I'm so tired I don't think I can talk to anyone right now."

"Mr. Costa, I think you'd better take this call," she said.

I sat up. That sounded ominous. Maybe something had happened to one of my children or something had gone awry at work. I picked up the phone on the bedside table, a litany of dark possibilities scrolling through my mind.

"Hello?" I said.

"Victor?" It was a woman's voice, familiar and yet I couldn't pin down who it belonged to.

"Yes, this is Victor Costa."

"I just called to say I love you." The caller sang the first line of the Stevie Wonder song—and then kept going. A minute or so later, I realized it was Oprah Winfrey serenading me her thanks for my gift.

I saw photos of her at the event, glamorous and glowing in the deep forest-green dress and opera coat, punctuated by the stunning emerald and diamond jewelry. Of all the dresses a celebrity like Oprah could have chosen, she wore mine. I had to admit it was uncommonly satisfying. Some designers shrug it off when someone famous wears their clothes, like it's another day in the atelier, but they're pretending. Inside, they're jumping up and down, thrilled and amazed and wondering if something like that will happen again. Just like I did.

However, Oprah wasn't the first famous person who wore one of my designs. Over the years, I dressed celebrities like Meryl Streep, Ivana Trump, and Brooke Shields. Some former First Ladies also wore my designs, among them Betty Ford, Rosalynn Carter—who appeared at a White House event in one of my dresses without my even knowing it—and Lady Bird Johnson. But my biggest coup were the dresses I made for George H.W. Bush's inauguration in 1989.

After he won the election in 1988, I was contacted about designing gowns for some of the ladies attending the inaugural ceremony. I didn't dress Barbara Bush—she chose Arnold

Scaasi for her husband's big night—but I did make exquisite dresses for future First Lady Laura Bush and her twin daughters, Barbara and Jenna, who were youngsters then. I also made dresses for Margaret Crow, wife of Dallas real estate developer Trammel Crow, and the fashion director of the Dallas Apparel Mart. The big surprise was when Mrs. Crow invited me to attend the inauguration. I flew up to Washington, D.C., with the Crows on their company plane and had a marvelous time. What a gala! Not only did Michael Crawford—who sang the lead in *Phantom of the Opera* on Broadway—perform at the inaugural dinner, but I was seated next to Shirley Temple Black—yes, *that* Shirley Temple. It was a very grand, memorable evening.

One of the dearest friends I made during those go-go years was a fantastic lady named Nancy. I think we met through a mutual acquaintance, but who remembers? That's how long it has been. We hit it off, bonding over our shared love of clothes and art. If I had ten dollars for every time I made a friend through fashion, I'd be a rich man. In this case, however, Nancy had the money—many millions, in fact, that she inherited when her oilman husband died unexpectedly in 1985. A renowned philanthropist, she put that money to good work, donating generously to Dallas universities, and arts and cultural organizations. Nancy was also known for throwing memorable parties and for traveling in style, which is how I wound up attending the Royal Ascot race with her and her mother, who went by Mamacita.

I planned to be in Paris in July for a shopping trip around the same time, give or take a few days, as the famous race. When she found out I would be "in the neighborhood," Nancy invited me to be her escort to the day's events, which included a seat in the Royal Enclosure with members of the royal family. The way I saw it, London was on the way home, and Ascot was a short drive from London. I accepted the invitation; I may even have squealed a little with pleasure.

Ascot was a once-in-a-lifetime experience, a magical adventure I could never have imagined. I wore tails and a top hat, mingled with the who's who of English society, along with some of Dallas's social elite. Nancy, Mamacita, and I had such a ball that, once we were back home, I became Nancy's regular escort. We went to art openings, fundraisers, and galas together. No doubt tongues wagged across the Big D, speculating about what was happening between Nancy, who was at least twenty years older, and that younger fashion designer. We never had a physically intimate relationship. She alluded to the possibility enough that it got my attention, but I kept her at arm's length.

My experience with Dawn Mello taught me, among other things, that mixing sex and friendship was a bad idea. Someone usually got their feelings hurt or heart broken, and I made it clear to Nancy that I did not want to wreck our friendship by hopping into bed with her. She accepted our status quo, although I did occasionally catch her eyeballing me in a way that made me blush.

It was through Nancy that I met the actress Greer Garson, who was married to a millionaire lawyer from Dallas named Buddy Fogelson. Ms. Garson was one of the most charming women I've ever met. One year, she invited Nancy and me to visit their ranch in Pecos, New Mexico. We took a train from Dallas that made a special stop at the Forked Lightning Ranch before continuing on to Santa Fe.

I loved Ms. Garson's fiery red hair and her moxie—she had plenty of both. We got along so well that once we were back in Dallas, she asked me to make a couple of dresses for her. One was for a gala that Southern Methodist University was throwing in her honor for the numerous gifts she had made over the years. When I agreed (of course I agreed!) to make an unforgettable dress, she wasted no time telling me, "I want red." She chose a bilious red, still known as Garson red, that did nothing for her. Instead, I made a long, sleeveless flowing coat and dress in a resplendent emerald green that made her glorious red hair glow like lava. Being a woman of class and taste, she acted as if that green was her choice all along.

By 1990, sales at the company hit nearly fifty million dollars. We had about twelve hundred accounts across four countries, including the major U.S. department stores, Harvey Nichols in London, Holt Renfrew in Toronto, and several department stores in Mexico. From the original womenswear and special occasion dresses, we expanded to include a bridal business, an accessories line, a girls' clothing line, and a suit collection called Tailleur. I even opened my first Victor Costa boutique in Highland Park Village in Dallas, where I kept company with high-end specialty stores like Lou Lattimer. I had the walls painted pink and hired a Cuban lady to manage it. To avoid violating the divorce agreement that gave ownership of my wholesale outlet store to my ex-wife, all of the merchandise at the boutique sold at full-retail price. That was a nice loophole.

With all that going on, I couldn't have been more surprised when Christian Dior contacted me about creating a secondary line for the U.S. market. They came to me because they knew I went to Paris at least twice a year to see and copy their designs, and I was reaping the publicity and profits. Why not copy for Dior legitimately? Why not, indeed? I loved the idea. I could make money and go through the archives at the House of Dior. It was a copyist's fantasy. I agreed, and they granted me the license to produce the Christian Dior America line. I gave it my all and did sales of three million dollars per year.

Unfortunately, that wasn't good enough for the *directrice* at Dior. I remember her response to some of my sketches—"They're very good, but they're too Dior."

"What do you mean, they're too Dior?" I practically spat out the words. "Isn't that what you hired me for?"

"We're going to do a full-page ad in *Vogue*, but you have to do something very simple," she said.

"That's not what Dior stands for," I protested.

But I did what she wanted. I made some pretty clothes, just not clothes I considered to be truly Dior. That arrangement lasted about a year before I gave it up. As much as I enjoyed being affiliated with a celebrated couture house and a creative director like Gianfranco Ferré, I didn't want—or need—to put up with their difficult *directrice*. More importantly, in 1990, I opened a branded Victor Costa boutique in Bergdorf Goodman. That helped take the sting out of walking away from Dior America.

Dawn Mello and I hadn't done much business together since the early 1970s, since she ghosted me after our affair. But in 1985, the organizers of the Metropolitan Museum Costume Institute Gala, known now as the Met Gala, chose me to design sari-inspired dresses for the windows at Bergdorf's because that year's theme was a salute to India. It broke the ice between Dawn and me. We weren't exactly bosom buddies again, but our once-close friendship was in a better place than it had been for years.

That's probably why Bergdorf's approached me about opening a Victor Costa boutique in the store. My New York sales manager Bob Miller and I met with store executives, conducted site visits, and finally hammered out a contract that mostly benefited Bergdorf's, but I was over the moon. For me, this was it, the pinnacle of my success: a branded boutique in the most exclusive department store in the U.S.

The cost of the build-out was two hundred and fifty thousand dollars. Per our agreement, once the boutique was up and running, Bergdorf's would take a percentage of every invoice from the Victor Costa boutique until the build-out was paid for. It was a spectacular space on the fourth floor overlooking the Plaza Hotel. And we owned that floor. When I flew in for personal appearances, throngs of women showed up. They came to see me and my designs, and Bob couldn't have been happier. As the face of Victor Costa, Inc., in New York, he interacted with customers and made everything flow smoothly, from the showroom to final sales. When the boutique at Bergdorf's opened, Bob was there nearly every Saturday to make sure shoppers enjoyed blue-chip service.

Of course, I probably wouldn't have had a boutique at Bergdorf's if it weren't for Dawn. She had left for a top job at Gucci by the time my boutique opened, but she lured me in and got the ball rolling. We did about three to four million dollars in sales a year in that location, which is undoubtedly why Bergdorf's wanted to keep taking a percentage of invoices even after the cost of the build-out was all paid up. They wouldn't budge, I refused to continue paying, and that was the end of our relationship. While I hoped it would last longer, I felt fortunate to have been a star in the Bergdorf's firmament, if only for a few years.

One year, my friend Ann Keenes invited me to the Met Gala. A sharp-witted redhead whose soft-spoken demeanor fooled more than one cocky designer, Ann had exited a top post at Neiman Marcus after many years to be vice president at Saks Fifth Avenue. The night of the gala, as we waited in the receiving line to greet the event chairs, I saw Oscar de la Renta standing near the entrance, probably waiting for his wife. It was no secret that I copied his designs every chance I got. Oscar made exquisite clothes; I tweaked them a little—some might say not at all—and made them much more affordable. Word was that my copies also tweaked his ego; that's how good they were.

Ann and I inched our way toward the head of the line, celebrity-spotting and admiring the lavish outfits. A Chanel here, a Valentino there, followed by Givenchy, Prada, Dior,

Armani, and more—it was a spectacle of couture fantasy from all the great fashion houses. That's when I heard Oscar single me out in a voice loud enough to turn heads.

"Victor," he said. "When are you going to start sending me royalties for copying my dresses?"

If he wanted to embarrass me, he failed. The entire world knew I copied his clothes; there was no crime in that. I acknowledged his comment with a genial nod and prepared to move into the throng when Ann spoke up.

"Want to know what I think, Oscar?" she trilled in her best cocktail-party voice. "I think Victor is going to do that when you start paying royalties to Dior and Saint Laurent."

It was one hell of a touché, punctuated by a few gasps and giggles among the guests in line behind us. Ever aware of appearances, Oscar laughed it off as if it were friendly banter between fellow designers. I could not have dreamed up a better way to start the evening.

Around that time, *New York Times* fashion critic Bernadine Morris, whom I'd known since my days in New York, came down to Dallas with fashion photographer Bill Cunningham to do a story on how things had gone for me since leaving New York and going out on my own. She wrote a very nice article that featured, among other things, a prominent sidebar about jackets. Bill lined up photos of very similar-looking jackets designed by Saint Laurent, Oscar de la Renta, and me. The headline encouraged readers to match the jacket to the designer.

I don't know if anyone ever wrote Bernadine with an answer, but people I knew who read the article told me they couldn't tell the difference between the Saint Laurent original, Oscar's copy of Saint Laurent, or my copy of Oscar. Therein lay the beauty of being, as John Fairchild, former publisher and editor of *Women's Wear Daily*, put it: "the best copyist in the world." My jacket looked like its couture cousins, but sold for much less. I wondered how Oscar felt about that.

CHAPTER 19

Clay and I had a good life in Dallas. Despite my hectic work and travel schedule, we made time for each other and our interests. We enmeshed ourselves in the social whirl of Dallas, hosting luncheons and fundraisers at our home in Highland Park. It's probably the exhibitionist in me, but if you have a pretty house, why not open the doors and let people have a peek? We loved pulling out all the stops for a large gathering or an intimate dinner, and I reveled in the compliments and praise that followed. Truth is, I have never been shy or retiring or secretive. Ask anyone who knows me. My life was an open book for nearly everyone. Except my mother.

As much as she loved me and inspired me to succeed, Mary Candelari Costa was a conservative Catholic woman raised in the 1920s; she would not have understood my relationship with Clay. Besides, people didn't flaunt their private lives in public with the same heedless enthusiasm as they do today. Clay and I agreed that whenever she came to visit, he would stay with his mother across town and come home when the coast was clear. Maybe it was gutless of me, but I didn't see how any good would come from being that honest and open with my mother. In this case, ignorance really was bliss.

And business kept booming. At the peak of my success, I had six different lines of clothing, including high-end womenswear, bridal, the less expensive Victor Costa Boutique, and, briefly, Christian Dior America. There were also a few years when my evening gowns and party frocks were all the rage with debutantes, prom queens, and gala chairs across Texas. I had a showroom in New York on Seventh Avenue and a one-bedroom apartment on the Upper East Side. In Dallas, I shared a big, fabulous house with Clay and a Cavalier King Charles Spaniel named Dior. That Highland Park house was my pride and joy. We filled it with antiques and decorated it in Delft blue and white. It was such a beauty that Neiman Marcus had a fashion show in our backyard, featuring Revillon furs and evening dresses from my womenswear collection.

I should have been happy with my business and my accomplishments in fashion; I should have been overjoyed. But I wanted to prove to myself—and possibly the world—that there was no limit to what I could achieve. If I had stopped grasping for more and more, things might have turned out differently. I didn't, though, and my life changed course as a result. Fortunately, I subscribe to the existential idea that everything happens for a reason. Otherwise, who knows where I might have ended up?

The thread of my carefully constructed life started to unravel in the early nineties when I discovered that John, my CFO, had been embezzling from the company, conning both me and our accounting firm. My daughter, Adrienne, who worked at the company for a while, told me she didn't trust him. She couldn't put her finger on why, but she had a feeling. "There's something off about him, Daddy," she said. I should have listened to her. John must have known she was onto him because he fired her, claiming that she often distracted other employees during work hours. My objection to her dismissal was lackluster. I was concerned about appearances, and I didn't want to be accused of nepotism. Worse, I gave him the credit I should have given Adrienne. On paper, we were making so much money that I went along with what he said was best for the business. And it got me royally screwed. Ultimately it was my own fault because I should have known better. I should have listened to my daughter, but I didn't until it was too late.

John was the young man I'd hired in 1985. He oversaw our finances, ensured everything came in on budget, balanced the books, and worked closely with a national accounting firm that had offices in Dallas and conducted certified public audits of my company. According to him, we were doing everything right and had plenty of money in the bank. The more business I brought in, the better; he assured me that we could handle it. As far as I knew, all was well. Until the day I found out, quite by accident, that it wasn't.

At first, it seemed like nothing. Small things, a trail of breadcrumbs I didn't have the sense to recognize or follow. Every now and then, John asked if he could use the company credit card for personal expenses like buying steaks or stopping for dinner on his way home from the office. He worked long hours, so I gave him wiggle room to treat himself and his family. And that's what he did. He treated himself to groceries and restaurant meals; he leased cars, bought clothes for his wife, and charged up a fortune in furniture for their new house. I had no idea this was going on until the credit card company called to tell me that I was three months behind on paying my bill.

I had no doubt this was a mistake. Our financial situation had gotten a little tight between up-front costs for several collections and collecting payment from clients, but I thought—no, I was sure—we had enough. As John happened to be in New York on business, staying in the company apartment, I asked my assistant to pull the statements so I could review them. She came in with a stack of paper and handed me half.

"These are the bills you paid," she said. "And here are the bills you haven't paid." She handed me the rest of the stack.

I paged through the unpaid bills and saw an unfamiliar card number on the statements, not my company card number. When I couldn't track John down, I went to his office and told his secretary I wanted a look at the records.

"Where are these records?" I asked, waving the unpaid

statements at her. "I want to see these records."

"There's a cabinet in his office where he keeps files," she said. "But that's his private cabinet."

"Where are the keys?" I demanded.

"He doesn't let anybody into that cabinet, not even me," she said.

That's when I reached my boiling point. I left, returned with a sledgehammer I probably borrowed from the building's maintenance supervisor, and proceeded to break open the private cabinet in John's office. Inside were records, statements, and stacks of cash, money (it turned out) he had siphoned off to help build and furnish the house I thought his father-in-law was bankrolling. While I was out drumming up new business, meeting with private clients, and designing new collections, my CFO was falsifying records, using a credit card on my company account, and robbing me blind.

I called the police and filed a complaint. When John returned from New York, building security escorted him out. I intended to press charges and put him away, but first I wanted to speak with the white-shoe accounting firm that, despite conducting regular audits of my company and meetings with my CFO, had been hoodwinked. I met with their representatives at my house in Highland Park on a Sunday afternoon. I went into that meeting angry, with visions of a lawsuit or some other legal recourse; by the time they left, I was utterly deflated and demoralized. It was clear that none of us realized that John had been embezzling right under our noses.

In the end, he made off with about three-quarters of a million dollars. That doesn't seem like a huge amount in terms of today's extraordinary wealth, but in the early 1990s it was big money for a company the size of mine. To this day, I don't know why I didn't press charges or go public about his crime. No doubt my ego played a role in that. Embarrassed, I walked away.

In the aftermath of that episode, you'd think I would have

been more attuned to what was happening around me, more adept at reading signs or tea leaves. Sadly, no. John's betrayal left me unable to see past the end of my nose. How could I possibly keep my eyes on any ball? My company's finances were, at that point, in a delicate state, but we had more than enough work and clients to keep things going, so much so that I hired a former industry acquaintance to be my production director. Bob, who worked for many years at Jerry Silverman, Inc., was enjoying retirement in California. He had a reputation for being professional, meticulous, and exacting, the kind of person I wanted to oversee production, watch the patterns, and ensure that everything was cut and made properly. When I heard he was coming to Dallas for a visit, I invited him to stop by my office. I laid out what I was looking for, asked him to come on board as my production director, and, in a fit of desperate exuberance, told him to name his salary. He did, I agreed, and he promptly accepted the job. Maybe retirement wasn't that fabulous, after all.

The "friend" he was visiting turned out to be a hairdresser named Chuck, who worked at a chic Dallas salon. Chuck was bosom buddies with an attractive young woman named Laura, who was that salon's front-desk receptionist. When she found out that Bob worked for a fashion designer, she asked him to recommend her as a fitting model.

A fitting model is a live mannequin—in this case, a woman—who works with a fashion designer and tries on new garments in various stages of construction to check the fit, the drape of the fabric, and generally how the piece looks. Think Elsa Peretti and Halston. I didn't have Elsa; I had Elaine. She was a fine fitting model, a size eight with a bosom, a waist, and curves. I never used stick figures because my customers were real women, not runway models. I wanted to keep Bob happy, so I gently broke the news to Elaine that I wouldn't be able to use her anymore. She couldn't have been more gracious.

Several phone calls and a meeting later, I hired Laura, a decision I would come to regret.

It is standard industry practice to fit a piece before it goes into production. With Elaine, I fitted for a size eight, and the production people graded the patterns up in size from there. Laura was a size six, which precipitated a minor change in the fitting and grading routine. I paid her thirty-five dollars an hour to come in two or three times a week when I needed her for fittings. Things hummed along smoothly for several months, until one day I noticed the dresses were a little snug on her. Tighter than the previous week or the week before that.

"Laura, we fitted this last week and made some corrections," I pointed out. "This is the corrected piece, and it's so tight we can barely zip it up. What's going on?"

She hesitated, then confessed to being several months pregnant. I couldn't believe it. I sent my reliable fitting model packing, only to have her replacement unable to work. Out went Laura to gestate while I found a temporary substitute. She eventually had the baby, slimmed back down to a size six, and returned to work a few months later. Laura had been working for me for a little over a year when she came into my office one day and asked for a full-time job. She said she struggled to control her spending; the minute she got a paycheck, she went out and spent it. Part-time work didn't cover the bills—well, it wouldn't if she was blowing her money on cocktails and clothes, would it? She really needed a full-time salary. Could I help?

It wasn't the ideal time to ask. In the intervening months since she had exited to have her baby and returned, my company's financial situation had gone from not great to worse. I was under pressure to produce, pay bills, and make money. I didn't handle the stress well. My temper flared occasionally, and I probably shouted more often than I should have.

But I don't recall behaving like a monster. Nor did I sexually harass any of my employees. Those close to me knew I would never do something so disrespectful. When I told Laura that I couldn't afford to hire her full-time, she flounced right out of the office and didn't come back. I was secretly relieved; she turned out to be a mediocre fitting model and had become increasingly difficult to work with. I didn't think much of it until my receptionist buzzed me one day not long after Laura quit.

"There's a call for you, Mr. Costa," she said. "I think you'd better take it."

Puzzled, I answered my phone. The next thing I knew, a male voice on the other line accused me of sexually harassing Laura.

"Your life as you know it is going to change," the caller continued. "We're going to sue you and get every penny you have. If you can cough up some money, we'll drop all of this."

It was extortion, plain and simple. I should have gone to the *Dallas Morning News* and told them the story of how my ex-employee was falsely accusing me of something and trying to get me to pay her to keep quiet and go away. Instead, the effrontery of it got under my skin enough. When he called again to discuss the terms of their extortion, I told him to go ahead and sue me. A few weeks later, a friend of mine called one morning to report what I should have expected all along: Laura and her attorney told the newspaper that I forced her to quit and she was suing me for sexual harassment and verbal abuse.

Me? Sexually harass a woman? Didn't they know I was in a relationship with a man? The idea would have been laughable if she wasn't looking for five million dollars in punitive damages. Five million dollars. I didn't have that kind of money. And, by the way, I did not sexually harass her. If anything, she flirted with me, but I never rose to that bait. It was late 1993, and I was embroiled in a lawsuit, spending money I didn't have to defend myself, and losing my grip on a company I had worked years to build.

In 1994, as Laura's lawsuit dragged on and our respective attorneys lined up character witnesses, JCPenney contacted me about producing a new line called Romantica. My first inclination was to dismiss the idea. A retailer that catered more to the masses and not my usual audience probably wasn't a good fit. But as I considered the pros and cons and negative publicity from Laura's accusations, I decided that if I adjusted my expectations and designed for their shoppers, we could reap some benefits, namely positive coverage and new customers. My industry friends wrinkled their noses at the idea, but they weren't in my shoes. We lost a few big accounts; some retailers were acquired and shut down, while others simply stopped carrying my lines. The hard truth was that my company needed the business. JCPenney and I signed an agreement, and production for Romantica began.

Meanwhile, my sweet, generous friend Nancy insisted on loaning me two hundred and fifty thousand dollars to help keep my company from sinking under the weight of attorney's fees and production costs. I thought surely that kind of cash infusion would provide the cushion we needed to get us through this thorny patch. By late 1994, however, it was clear that Romantica at JCPenney was already at death's door—I did say their customers weren't our customers, didn't I?—and no amount of wishful thinking was going to keep my company in the black. It was, in fact, teetering on the edge of insolvency. My own finances were in an equally sad state, thanks to paying hundreds of thousands of dollars to the lawyers. But the final straw was when the judge hearing the lawsuit allowed Laura's claim of more than one and a half million dollars in actual damages to go through. That's when I knew beyond optimism and naïveté that this chapter of my life had come to a close.

In January 1995, I filed for Chapter 11 personal bankruptcy;

two months later, I closed down our corporate showroom in New York. In June, I filed for Chapter 7 protection, effectively shutting down my company for good. As I remember that dark period in my life, I can see where I went wrong, what I should have done, what I did and did not do—perhaps with a more objective, experienced eye. Back then, however, I was destroyed, shocked, and furious as much with myself as with those who betrayed me.

One of my biggest regrets is that I was too much of an artist and not more of a businessman. I thought I didn't need to mind my business; after all, I was so great, talented, and untouchable, right? My arrogance cost me my company and my reputation. But like the perennials I planted in the flower beds at my Highland Park house, I intended to grow back.

Not long after shutting down Victor Costa, Inc., I signed on with the A.S. Design Group at 501 Seventh Avenue, once the site of my own showroom. A multiple-line sales company, A.S. Design took on the responsibility of showing my collection in regional markets as well as in Dallas, Atlanta, and Los Angeles. I already had a new line ready to go when I closed my company. It just needed a home.

Clay and I decamped to a small West Side apartment I'd leased several years earlier since I traveled to New York so often for business. Despite having closed my company, I kept the apartment, unsure where we would land and how long we might be there. It turned out to be a smart move because I stayed at A.S. Design for two years. That's when my friend Ann Keenes, whose contacts in the fashion industry were legend, asked if I was interested in meeting with a Korean man named Cho. He owned a manufacturer that produced cheap clothing and was looking to bring a touch of class to his company.

"Mr. Cho wants to put you back in business," she said.

I loved the sound of that. As long as someone else was in charge of the business side of things, I was willing to consider a variety of design jobs. At that point, what did I have to lose? I agreed to meet with Mr. Cho. To my surprise, he turned out to be a big fan of my dresses and wanted me to take over as head designer for his company's eveningwear division. The offer included a very good salary and moving expenses. Was it a dream job? Definitely not. I had that and lost it. But sometimes you take what you can get, and sometimes good enough is all you need to start over. I accepted the job and, in a few months, moved back to New York.

PART FOUR:

Back to New York, 1995-2012

CHAPTER 20

It didn't take long for me to realize that I wasn't cut out for full-time apartment living. With Clay and me tripping over each other in the small confines of our one-bedroom and the smell of last night's dinner lingering for days in the kitchen, I yearned for good ventilation and more space. Now that I had money coming in, I was ready to find a house.

A lush garden. Winding country roads. Maybe even a rambling lawn. I wanted all of that and more. I settled on looking in Connecticut, which was close enough to commute but far enough from the twenty-four-hour frenzy of New York to offer tranquility and bucolic scenery.

Here's the other thing: I missed my furniture. The house in Highland Park sold quickly, and nearly everything in it was now sitting in a storage unit somewhere in Dallas. I wanted to see my things—the dining table and chairs, the antique sideboard, the exquisite sofas covered in fabric that cost nine hundred dollars a yard, all of it—artfully placed in a house again.

After many months of searching, I found a house in Sherman, Connecticut. It sat at the bottom of a hill, and it had a pretty garden and apple trees on the property. Best of all, it was on the market for three hundred thousand dollars, a price I could afford. Sherman is a small town with a population of about three thousand five hundred. It sits near the border with New York state, close to the town of Pawling, where all kinds of famous people had—and still have—homes. Moving my furniture to the house in Sherman cost Mr. Cho about thirty-eight thousand dollars. That's a lot of money now; nearly thirty years ago, it was a damn fortune. But he paid it without a whimper, and soon we made the house our home. I hung onto the New York City apartment for another couple of years, staying there several nights a week when I was working at Mr. Cho's company. Having a place in the city was a convenient luxury, but I couldn't really afford three thousand dollars a month in rent if someone else wasn't paying for it. Victor Costa, Inc., had covered the cost; Mr. Cho wasn't about to do the same. Eventually, and with much regret, I let the apartment go.

Clay, in the meantime, had been working off and on in New York for the fabled decorator Mario Buatta. My friend Sheila, who married and divorced a philandering Frenchman, helped him get the job. I met Sheila in Paris when I first started my company, and we hit it off instantly. She began coming to Texas for fun during her visits to the U.S. and would stay with Clay and me. What a charming, witty woman and a magnificent cook!

She also happened to be pals with Mario Buatta. When Clay told her he wanted to be a decorator, she called Mario and asked him to hire someone she knew who wanted experience and guidance in the interior design and decoration business. As Sheila liked to say, a handsome young man is always in demand. Clay worked as Mario's assistant for a while, maybe a year or two, until I gave up the New York lease and he decided the commute wasn't worth it. Instead, he made a point of getting to know Sherman and its residents through his involvement in civic and social groups, a smart move that would serve him well in the years to come.

My stint at Mr. Cho's company lasted two years, but they were interesting times. Among the most adventurous, at least for me, was when the U.S. Department of Agriculture arranged for a group of us to tour China, Japan, and South Korea. The goal was to promote homegrown U.S. cotton for export. I traveled with a collection of fifty Victor Costa dresses, all of them made of American cotton and printed in Asia. Magnificent prints. It was amazing, fascinating, like nothing I had ever done. Our group traveled from place to place on a train, taking in the sights, meeting with government officials, and promoting U.S. cotton. Everywhere we stopped, I found ceramics and dishes and decorative items I wanted to buy. The U.S. trade representative assigned to squire us around China offered to have everything shipped home for me, so I went wild. I bought a set of blue and white china for forty people. In China. I thought it was funny at the time.

Mr. Cho sent me to China and Hong Kong several times. He wanted to show me that China, not India, was the place to have clothing made. I remember the first time I went to Hong Kong with him, we traveled in first class. He wasn't cheap, I'll give him that. Then again, maybe that was his downfall. There were three of us: Mr. Cho, me, and his sister-in-law, who worked for the company. Apparently, everyone—except me— knew that he cheated on his wife with her sister, but I saw it happen in real time when I accidentally spotted her giving him a hand job under her coat. In first class! I saw my boss in a whole new light after that.

The good life didn't last long with Mr. Cho. Things went downhill when one of his business associates convinced him to buy another clothing company. In my opinion, there was some misrepresentation of the company's sales and financial health, but mostly it was a bad deal—and Mr. Cho fell for it, largely, I think, motivated by greed. On the books, it looked like the company he acquired did great business; however, that turned out to be a red herring, and he ran out of money not long after the acquisition. In June 1999, Mr. Cho's company declared bankruptcy. It was a shame, not only because I was out of work again, but also because Mr. Cho had provided me with a beautiful design facility around the corner from the showroom. I could recreate a dress design from ten years ago because I had all my models on microfilm. Believe it or not, that was cutting edge.

During my time working for Mr. Cho, I became a regular in the Saks Fifth Avenue Folio catalog, which was discontinued in 2001. For many years, however, it operated independently of the store, with models, clothing lines, and products that were unique to the catalog. I did a robust business with Saks Folio, designing exclusive lines and pieces for them. It was good for me and great for the company. When Mr. Cho announced the bankruptcy, I swung into action to get my designs out of the office and into my briefcase. It was the first thing I thought of. Call me ruthless, but I had been through enough by then to know better.

The day we were supposed to vacate the building, Mr. Cho's sister-in-law—the same one he was sleeping with—came down to my office. Fortunately, I was there going through my files and packing my samples and books—that is, my original designs as well as bound copies of my collections—when she waltzed in and began going through the remaining books on the shelf and pulling them down.

"What are you doing?" I asked.

"You're not taking all this information," she said in a snippy tone. "These are the company's property."

"Those are all mine," I said. "They have my name in them. I brought them in, and I'm taking them out. Get the fuck out of here."

I got a little rude, but the woman was trying to lay claim to my designs. Once I got all my samples and books out of there, I was stuck with a collection of clothing and no place to show it. If I had to do it over, I would have gone back into business under my own name. But at that time, I didn't want the headache. I found a company that took in all my samples because they were made and didn't cost them anything. In late 1999, I joined Rose Taft Couture, an eveningwear manufacturer with a showroom at 498 Seventh Avenue. They were looking for a contemporary line of dresses for younger customers, and my designs fit the bill. With them, I was able to launch the Victor Costa Collection because I had a line that was ready to go.

Rose Taft Couture was run by the founder's daughter. As far as I could tell, they charged five hundred dollars or more to make ugly dresses for the mother of the bride. Meanwhile, there I was with a new collection ready to go—all we needed was orders. The founder's son, who was a very handsome guy, said he wanted to build the Victor Costa name. I almost pointed out that my name had already been built and out there for a while, then thought better of it. The company had an enormous showroom, and I had the clothes. I made a few calls to Saks and a few other retailers—and we were back in business. Same customers, different company.

I stayed at Rose Taft from 1999 to 2002. It wasn't my favorite job, but it paid well enough and I had the freedom to design eveningwear lines under my name. In 2001, I got a call from QVC, one of the original television home shopping networks, asking if I wanted to produce a Victor Costa line for the under-forty crowd. Their audience skewed older, and they wanted to capitalize on younger women who weren't necessarily wealthy but had a little spending money. It was a big deal when QVC wanted to put you—in this case, me—on the air to sell your products. I figured it couldn't hurt to supplement my income from Rose Taft. Besides, this was an adventure I'd never had. And there was my compulsive need to be in constant motion.

Before I could sell anything on QVC, I had to attend a special training course. That seemed amusing at first, until I understood that producing clothes for QVC wasn't about whipping out a line and handing it off to a retailer. I was the designer and the salesman. I had a time slot on the show during which I was expected to perform and sell to an audience that was everywhere, all across the country. If I didn't generate enough in sales, they would show me the door. Politely, of course. I have to confess I didn't care for the network setting sales milestones and pressuring me to reach them. At first, I thought it was a strange way to do business. Then I reminded myself that times had changed, and I could change with them or find the nearest pasture. I chose to stick with it.

The Victor Costa Occasion collection launched in 2001. It was an eye-catching line of separates—jackets, tops, skirts, and such—inspired by my love of and familiarity with haute couture. The night of my debut, I didn't know what to expect: whether my clothes would sell or whether my sales spiel would fall flat. I went out there and talked to the viewers as if they were sitting in the room with me. I described what made each piece special, what to wear it with, how to accessorize it, and why it would make them feel like the star of their own show. It was like I had discovered a new world—and I loved it. Apparently, the ladies watching me loved it, too; by the time I got to the third item on my list, everything had sold out. I did one million dollars in sales in forty-seven minutes, breaking all the QVC records. At the end of the evening, all I had left was the smile on my face. Now that was something.

I couldn't have been more surprised. I'm no skeptic, not really. I hadn't expected to find a home at QVC, but it suited me well—well enough that when I left Rose Taft in 2002, I stayed on at QVC, commuting to company headquarters in Pennsylvania once a month for my television appearance. I made good money there and was a hit with the viewers, who I fondly referred to as my "club of ladies." My designs were so popular that I became a fixture at the network. At its peak, Victor Costa Occasion had one hundred thousand active shoppers and regularly sold two million dollars' worth of merchandise in an hour of airtime. My most devoted shoppers sent me hundreds of letters and pictures, thanking me for my designs and my fashion advice. I loved knowing I made their lives better in some way.

I was still at QVC when the CEO of Stein Mart contacted me in 2005 to see if I would design a dress and separates line for the discount store chain. He wanted a line of womenswear for Stein Mart's Ladies' Boutique collection, with the look and feel of couture, but at a price shoppers could afford. In other words, he hired me to do what I did best. That line debuted in a hundred Stein Mart stores in the summer of 2005 and expanded to the entire chain the following year.

When I wasn't working in my studio or displaying my designs on television, I tried to be an active resident of Sherman. Between brainstorming new collections and selling my designs on QVC, I didn't have a ton of free time. But I did want to get to know and connect with my community. One way I did that was by singing in the five o'clock mass on Saturdays at our local Catholic church. I was a choir of one, but the showman in me didn't mind one bit. Clay and I showed up every week, and I sang my heart out.

I even had a small fan club: two ladies who usually attended and sat together in one of the front pews. I thought maybe they came for the pleasure of hearing my voice, until I found out they were both Catholic. We finally got around to introducing ourselves one evening after mass. Katie and Dorrie had become friends through their husbands, who had also been friends. Now, they were a pair of wealthy widows—Katie's husband had been CEO of Citibank, while Dorrie's co-founded a major health insurance company—who spent part of the year in their grand second homes in Sherman.

They also happened to be interesting, intelligent, and lots of fun. Dorrie favored Chanel, raised Springer Spaniels, and threw fabulous Derby Day parties. I remember when she wanted to build a kennel for the dogs she was raising and breeding, and the town of Sherman wouldn't approve it because constructing a separate facility violated zoning laws. Not one to be stonewalled, Dorrie added the kennel onto the existing house instead. Clever woman. Katie was no shrinking violet, either. She liked to walk the perimeter of her sprawling property and, on occasion, could be spotted mowing the long grass herself, perched high on a tractor. Clay and I often had dinner with her after mass, and we would talk about everything from art and fashion to current events.

There was a third friend, another woman I hadn't yet crossed paths with. In fact, I had no idea who she was or what she looked like until I met her at a fundraising dinner in 2010. It was an elaborate annual event to raise money for the library in Pawling, New York. The evening began with a lecture at the library, then continued at various homes around town where people showed up for a catered dinner. I arrived at the library with Clay and the friends who invited us to hear a Beatles expert wax nostalgic about the band and its impact on music and popular culture. I've never been a Beatles fan, so I was relieved when his talk wrapped up and we left for the dinner, which he happened to be hosting at his house.

There were plenty of friends and neighbors wandering around, as we attended this event every year. But I was surprised to find that, when I took my seat at the dinner table, I did not know the woman sitting next to me. I did, however, recognize the jacket she was wearing, a crocheted work of art that had proved a welcome distraction from the dull lecture. I'd never seen a jacket that pretty. It practically sang to me.

As someone who produced a lot, I was always looking for something to copy, and I needed pieces to copy for QVC. It sounds like I had business on the brain, twenty-four hours a day, even at social gatherings. I didn't really, but when I saw something that triggered an idea, I ran with it. That happened to me more often than you'd think. For QVC, I could take a three-thousand-dollar jacket—and I was sure the jacket my lovely dinner partner wore cost at least that much—and make a near-perfect copy that retailed for about thirty-nine dollars. Incredible, right? The difference would be minimal. I could use the same material, have the jacket made in China, and the embroidery done in India. Expensive clothes are expensive because they don't make a lot of them.

I'll say this: the jacket made me swoon, but the woman wearing it—now that I was up close and personal—was even prettier than the jacket. She commanded my attention. Okay, I still wanted a look at the label; I had to know who made it. No better way to find out than by introducing myself.

"Hello, I'm Victor Costa." I leaned forward, hoping to spy a name on the label. No luck.

"Well, hello, Victor," she said with a strong hint of Texas in her voice. "My name is Jerry Ann Woodfin. I'm so pleased to meet you. I believe you know my friends Katie and Dorrie."

This was the third friend I'd never met. As if knowing what I was after, she grinned, leaned forward a little, and there it was: Oscar de la Renta. Of course. I smiled at her, this lovely woman with excellent taste in clothing, and understood in my bones that, while this might be our first encounter, it would certainly not be our last. Fate had brought us together. Well, fate and Oscar.

CHAPTER 21

The night I met Jerry Ann Woodfin felt like a fairy tale. There I was in upstate New York, out for an evening at someone's home, helping to raise money for a good cause. Everyone dressed up, laughing and chatting over cocktails and dinner. Seeing old friends and making new ones. Sitting next to an impeccably dressed woman with a thousand-watt smile—and a fabulous jacket. As I drove home that night, feeling unusually carefree and cheerful, I wondered if I was up to the task of juggling three women, two of whom seemed to have more than friendship on their minds and one who caught my attention and held it.

I know what you're thinking. Why was I flirting with three women when I already lived with someone? The truth is that somewhere in the back of my mind, I knew things with Clay wouldn't last. He was young, I was not. We had different interests and friends, different aspirations. There were so many differences. Besides, I had always loved women; I was very candid about that. Why wouldn't I have at least a few female friends? And why wouldn't I flirt with them? A little harmless flirtation didn't mean anything, right?

Not long before I met Jerry Ann, I sold our first house in Sherman, the one I loved best, for eight hundred thousand dollars—not bad, given that I'd paid three hundred thousand—and immediately bought another to avoid paying exorbitant taxes. The second house was a real beauty, a historic landmark that needed some renovation and tender loving care. But Clay didn't want to live in an antique; he preferred the contemporary houses popping up around town. In retrospect, I should have told him it wasn't his call; it was my money, and I wanted this house. As I had done so often in the past, I took the path of least resistance and gave in. I remember wondering when the hell I was going to do what I wanted, not what someone else demanded. I sold the historic house quickly and bought a very modern house that had a first-floor master suite and very little personality.

In 2010, I was still at QVC, producing womenswear and money for the company and connecting with my "club of ladies." I was having a ball at work. Clay handled all the marketing for my brand, including social media, which was breaking out as the next big thing. While it wasn't a full-time job, he had other commitments to keep him busy and involved, including serving on the town Planning and Zoning Commission, the Zoning Board of Appeals, and the Historic District Commission. He even spearheaded the expansion and renovation of the Sherman Public Library. I was both proud and envious of his limitless energy for working a day job and devoting himself to civic work. Then again, he was young, and I was not.

I assumed Clay would keep racking up projects and kudos until he discovered what he really wanted to do. Katie and Jerry Ann, however, had other plans for him. They'd heard me express frustration more than once about how a young man his age, with so much life ahead of him, should have a purpose and a career. They must have listened and decided to do something, because in 2011 Clay was approached by several of the town's wealthy residents about running for first selectman, or mayor, of Sherman. That he already had some experience with town politics from serving on the Planning and Zoning Commission was a big plus. What he needed was money to fund a campaign. That's where Jerry Ann and Katie came in.

Money. Supposedly it's the root of all evil, and yet you

can't run a political campaign without it. Those two ladies pulled out their checkbooks without a second thought. With their money—and there was a lot of it—Clay rented a former antique shop to serve as his campaign headquarters. The front of the space was all glass, and we hosted pizza parties every Wednesday night. People walking by stopped in for a free slice and got a pitch from Clay in the deal. We printed flyers and put up a giant billboard on the road from Sherman to Pawling. There was his face, larger than life, with *Vote for Clay* printed across the bottom. He was literally all over in town. With that kind of money and publicity, how could he lose?

He couldn't. And he didn't. I remember the night my partner was elected first selectman of Sherman. It was a hard-fought election for a small town, but he received the most votes. His campaign volunteers could not have been happier. As I watched them hustle Clay out of campaign headquarters to celebrate with his supporters and fans, it dawned on me in that moment that my life was changing. He would work all day, and I would take care of him, as he had taken care of me for the past twenty-five years. That's how long we had been together, and I'd never really looked after him. In any secure, happy relationship, that role reversal would have felt right, but it didn't feel like a good fit to me.

As first selectman, Clay ran the town. He worked all the time, day and night, because a CEO is never really off-duty. I would be the first to say that he was an excellent selectman. Honest and earnest, he took the job very seriously. He cared about the town, and he poured his heart and soul into getting things done. After the election, I rarely saw him. Since I was at QVC only once or twice a month, I became something of a homebody, while Clay worked all hours. Even if I had dinner ready for him, he was often so exhausted after a long day that he would go straight to bed without eating. While I cared about his well-being, it didn't escape me that we were living separate lives. And I didn't mind.

*

In the meantime, I got closer to Katie and Jerry Ann. I liked Katie—she was fun to be with and a terrific date—but Jerry Ann had a certain spark. I couldn't explain why she lit me up inside; it was a wonderful feeling. Katie didn't think it was so great—my pleasure in Jerry Ann's company must have shown on my face—and she let me know in a way that told me she was not happy.

One evening, the three of us were at a party in Sherman, and I was chatting with a priest about the possibility of having my first marriage annulled; how the process worked and whether it was even feasible (it wasn't, so the annulment never happened). Maybe my subconscious mind knew I wanted the option of getting married again. Who knows? Jerry Ann and Katie joined us in time to catch the tail end of our conversation. Next thing I knew, Katie turned to Jerry Ann and said, "If Victor gets an annulment, he's going to marry me. Not you." Flattering as that was, I knew, or at least suspected, that Jerry Ann had already won that battle without firing a single shot.

Then there was the night of the Fireman's Ball. I had already agreed to escort Katie, when Jerry Ann invited me to attend another event the same evening, but at a later time. Foolishly, I figured I could juggle both women and events, with no fallout. As Katie and I walked into the ball, I chose that moment to say, "I'm not sure how long I can stay because I'm meeting Jerry Ann at nine o'clock." Why was I surprised when she hauled off and elbowed me in the stomach hard enough that I had to catch my breath? I couldn't blame her; my behavior was rude and addled, like that of a besotted teenage boy.

Any romantic designs Katie had on me came crashing down. It was just as well. I was still living with and providing for Clay, but I only had eyes for Jerry Ann. Turned out she had a thing for me, too. The two of us began going to dinner and the theater and enjoying each other's company in her gorgeous home in Pawling. Increasingly, I felt like I was being pulled in opposite directions. Did Clay notice me withdrawing? Probably not at first. He put work above everything like I did, and he didn't have much time or energy for anything else.

On the occasional weekends he did have free, we made plans with friends. One night we were at Jerry Ann's house for dinner, always an elegant affair, and Clay wanted to go home early. I told him to take the car, that I would see him later. At the end of our evening, I borrowed one of Jerry Ann's cars to get home. As I walked in the door, Clay was coming down the stairs.

"Whose BMW is that?" he asked, peering through one of the sidelights.

"It's Jerry Ann's," I answered. "I'm going to bed." It was four o'clock in the morning.

That year—it was 2011—we were invited to a New Year's Eve party. The hosts were friends of Clay's, and the house was packed wall-to-wall with young people. I remember sitting on the sofa, chatting with a woman and knowing I didn't belong in that crowd. Clay was young; I was not. He had his life stretching out ahead of him; I did not. After all those years together, the age difference finally mattered.

In the summer of 2012, Jerry Ann threw a party on her terrace. There was live music and cocktails and gourmet food. I remember the moment like a snapshot in time: the band was playing "Night and Day," but nobody was dancing. Jerry Ann grabbed my hand—the woman loves to dance—and led me to the dance floor. I'm good on my feet, and we were having a ball, twirling one minute, cheek to cheek the next. One dance, then another and another, and still we were the only pair out there. A friend of hers came up after a few songs and tapped me on the shoulder.

"You'd better break this up," she said. "You're causing trouble."

I supposed she meant that Clay was there, and people were starting to talk. Jerry Ann was having none of that.

"Get out of here," she told her friend. "We are having fun. Why shouldn't we?"

As her friend slouched back to the gossiping crowd, I looked at Jerry Ann.

"Looks like we're causing trouble," I said.

"It sure does." She smiled. "I don't know what to do."

"Well, maybe we should get married," I suggested.

"Maybe that's a good idea," she said.

That night was my last in the modern house with the ground-floor master bedroom. I returned to Jerry Ann's house the next day and never went home again. Coward that I was, I didn't tell Clay I was moving out; instead, I called one of his close friends and asked him to give Clay the bad news.

"Tell him he can have everything in the house, all the furniture, china, antiques, and paintings," I said. "I don't want any of it."

This was the end, and I didn't want to bring anything from the old relationship into the new one. I wanted a fresh start, a clean slate, all those clichés you've heard but not thought much about. They suddenly meant a lot to me. I walked away and left everything behind, the accumulation of a lifetime. I don't know how Clay reacted—he's a smart guy, so he probably saw it coming. I chose not to see or speak with him; I wanted a clean break and, yes, I was also avoiding the confrontation and a drawn-out goodbye. A few days later, while he was at work, I picked up my clothes and a few personal items. On the way out, I left my keys in the front hall and closed the door.

Jerry Ann and I skipped the whole engagement part and cruised straight to married. We went to the Pawling town hall and got a marriage license. Then we called a friend, who happened to be a justice of the peace, and booked a wedding date. I had seen a Chanel jacket during one of our shopping trips and bought it for her, so I went to one of my favorite fabric stores in New York City, bought some silk crepe, and made a skirt to match the jacket. The result was an elegant outfit for my bride. The day of our wedding—September 7, 2012—I drove to a local greenhouse, cut some of their exquisite orchids, and made a bouquet.

We were married on the terrace of her house, with Barbara—then a division president at Chanel—as maid of honor and her husband, John—former chairman of Bonwit Teller and I. Magnin—as my best man. Our friends Peter and Dana, who was a Broadway performer, were also there. After the ceremony, a huge tin of caviar and lots of Dom Pérignon awaited us on the terrace. However, I cooked the wedding feast—homemade sauce and pasta for everyone—just as I'd done for my fellow Pratt students decades earlier. Dessert was a croquembouche, a tower of French pastry puffs held together with caramel. What a happy, delicious day that was!

The one thing we didn't do was tell Jerry Ann's children or mine. We weren't being secretive or sly, and we weren't keeping anything from them. We would tell them—sooner, rather than later—but this day, this ceremony, belonged to us and nobody else, and that's how we played it.

In the midst of making our plans, QVC called to tell me they were going to cut my hours. I would be on three times a year, instead of once a month. If that's not a sign to move on, I don't know what is. When I told Jerry Ann of those impending changes, she looked pleased.

"I don't want you to do that anymore," she said. "In fact, I don't want you to work at all. I want you to be with me."

"Well, I don't know..." I said.

"How about this?" she said. "I've got us two first-class tickets to Paris, and we're going next week."

I'd have been a fool to turn that down. Just like that, I was a retired fashion designer. No longer a copycat, but a doting husband, a partner in shopping, a date to all manner of grand cultural events. To think it all started with a jacket.

I never expected to find myself back in Houston. We kept the house in Pawling and an apartment on the Upper East Side, but my wife is a Houston girl through and through. After we married, we bought a house near the twelfth tee of the Houston Country Club golf course. We spend six months a year in New York, with weekends in Pawling and weekdays in Manhattan going to concerts, the theater, and out for gourmet meals. We also spend six months in Houston, attending galas and fundraisers and seeing friends, her children, and grandchildren. I don't see my children as often as I'd like, since they live on either coast, but I keep in touch regularly.

We are so busy that there's no time for the grass to grow under my Gucci loafers. It's an extraordinary life I never thought I'd have. Who expects to find love again at the age of seventy-two?

When we first married, Jerry Ann would go up to New York and buy head-to-toe Oscar de la Renta. Given what she was wearing the first time we met, I knew she liked Oscar's clothes well before I swooped into her life. Now she has sentimental reasons for wearing them. I love shopping with her. Once when we were in Bergdorf's, I bought her a dress that impressed even the salesgirl.

"Where'd you find that?" she asked.

"I'm shopping for my wife," I said. "And trust me, I know how to shop."

It was a Carolina Herrera, a sheer coup de velour, and it looked divine on Jerry Ann. Even so, my suggestions don't always carry much weight; my wife has a mind of her own, especially when it comes to her closet. "I'll wear what I want to wear" is one of her favorite sayings, and she means it. But she still has a salesperson at Bergdorf's who keeps an eye out for new fashions from her favorite designers, and she still buys Oscar.

I did very well and enjoyed great success in my life, especially for a boy from the wrong side of town, but in many respects I think of myself as a failure. I got divorced, lost my company, and never made it to the level of a Karl Lagerfeld or Yves Saint Laurent. I was a mediocre father and a credulous, arrogant businessman. I could have done better and been better.

In the end, however, I did okay. To be called the best in the world at something is a big deal by any measure. And for a while, I was known as the best in the world at copying couture designs, an accomplishment I will always be proud of. Well, that and my ability to spot an Oscar de la Renta across a crowded room.

ACKNOWLEDGEMENTS

I would like to thank my children, Adrienne and Kevin, for giving me the *raison d'etre* to be successful and provide for them. I'd also to thank Cristina Adams, who wrote my life onto the page. Most of all, I am grateful to my beautiful wife, Jerry Ann, whose encouragement, kindness and understanding motivated me to pursue this passion project of mine to completion. I am hers forever.

About Atmosphere Press

Founded in 2015, Atmosphere Press was built on the principles of Honesty, Transparency, Professionalism, Kindness, and Making Your Book Awesome. As an ethical and author-friendly hybrid press, we stay true to that founding mission today.

If you're a reader, enter our giveaway for a free book here:

SCAN TO ENTER
BOOK GIVEAWAY

If you're a writer, submit your manuscript for consideration here:

SCAN TO SUBMIT
MANUSCRIPT

And always feel free to visit Atmosphere Press and our authors online at atmospherepress.com. See you there soon!

About the Author

Victor Costa is a womenswear designer, famous for his flawless interpretations of haute couture fashions, whose career spanned more than sixty years. A former member of the Council of Fashion Designers of America, he has garnered numerous awards and accolades over the decades, including May Company Design award, American Printed Fabrics Council Tommy award, Dallas Fashion Award, University of Houston Distinguished Alumni Award and University of Syracuse Lifetime Achievement Award in Design, among others. Now retired, he and his wife, Jerry Ann, split their time between Houston, TX, Pawling, NY and New York City.